The Teaching of Ethics II

Legal Ethics and Legal Education

Michael J. Kelly

INSTITUTE OF
SOCIETY, ETHICS AND
THE LIFE
SCIENCES THE
HASTINGS
CENTER

Copyright © 1980 by the Institute of Society, Ethics and the Life Sciences

All rights reserved. No part of this book may be reproduced or transmitted in any form or by any means, electronic or mechanical, including photocopying, recording or by any information storage and retrieval system, without permission in writing from the Publisher.

The Hastings Center
Institute of Society, Ethics and the Life Sciences
360 Broadway
Hastings-on-Hudson, New York 10706

Library of Congress Cataloging in Publication Data

Kelly, Michael J
   Legal ethics and legal education

   (The Teaching of ethics ; 2)
   Bibliography: p.
   1. Legal ethics—Study and teaching–United States.
   I. Title. II. Series: Teaching of ethics ; 2.
   KF277.L4K45   174'.3'071173   80–10825
   ISBN 0–916558–06–1

Printed in the United States of America

Contents

I.	Introduction	1
II.	A Brief History of Ethics in American Law Schools	5
III.	The Teaching of Ethics—1979	23
IV.	The Goals and Materials of the Ethics Course	29
	A. Subject Goals	29
	1. The Code of Professional Responsibility	29
	2. Role Morality	32
	(a) Zeal	33
	(b) Independent Judgment	33
	(c) Confidentiality	34
	3. The Disciplinary System	35
	4. The Profession and the Delivery of Legal Services	35
	B. Process Goals	37
	1. The Consensus	37
	2. The Activist Critique	39
V.	Recommendations	45
	A. The Materials for the Ethics Course	45
	1. Descriptive Ethics	47
	2. The Use of Theory	48
	B. The Course	48
	C. The Pervasive Method	50
	D. Clinics	51

VI. Conclusion 53
Notes 55
Selected Bibliography 65

FOREWORD

A concern for the ethical instruction and formation of students has always been a part of American higher education. Yet that concern has by no means been uniform or free of controversy. The centrality of moral philosophy in the undergraduate curriculum during the mid-nineteenth century gave way later during that century to the first signs of increasing specialization of the disciplines. By the middle of the twentieth century, instruction in ethics had, by and large, become confined almost exclusively to departments of philosophy and religion. Efforts to introduce ethics teaching in the professional schools and elsewhere in the university often met with indifference or outright hostility.

The past decade has seen a remarkable resurgence of interest in the teaching of ethics at both the undergraduate and professional school levels. Beginning in 1977, The Hastings Center, with the support of the Rockefeller Brothers Fund and the Carnegie Corporation of New York, undertook a systematic study of the teaching of ethics in American higher education. Our concern focused on the extent and quality of that teaching, and on the main possibilities and problems posed by widespread efforts to find a more central and significant role for ethics in the curriculum.

As part of that project, a number of papers, studies, and monographs were commissioned. Moreover, in an attempt to gain some degree of consensus, the authors of those studies worked together as a group for a period of two years. The study presented here represents one outcome of the project. We hope and believe it will be helpful for those concerned to advance and deepen the teaching of ethics in higher education.

Daniel Callahan   Sissela Bok
Project Co-Directors
The Hastings Center
Project on the Teaching of Ethics

About the Author

Michael J. Kelly

Michael J. Kelly is the Dean of the University of Maryland School of Law. He received his B.A. from Princeton, his Ph.D. in history from King's College, Cambridge University, and his LL.B. from Yale. Before his association with legal education, he served as counsel and aide to three mayors, Kevin White of Boston, and Thomas D'Alesandro and William Donald Schaefer of Baltimore.

I. Introduction*

Murray Schwartz, former dean and now Professor of Law at the University of California, Los Angeles, once delivered himself of an unusually pessimistic description of the role of American law schools in the moral development of future lawyers. He cited a number of factors that made legal education an "inhospitable" environment for the exploration of ethical issues: extraordinarily high faculty-student ratios that establish a distance between students and faculty; lack of a significant affective component in legal education other than intense emphasis on intellectual performance; faculty skeptical of their ability to affect the moral standards of students, in part because of a belief those standards are largely fixed by the time students reach law school; faculties largely comprised of nonpractitioners or expractitioners teaching as a result of their distaste for the ethics of practice; willingness of law schools to delay the socialization (i.e., basic professional formation) of lawyers to apprenticeship following the three years of legal education; and the "permissiveness" of the dominant set of ethical rules for lawyers in our country, the American Bar Association's Code of Professional Responsibility.[1] Schwartz developed a grim prognosis of the future of ethical training in law schools:

---

*I wish to thank David Franke, Robin West, Robert Shreve, and Jack Price, students at the University of Maryland Law School, who provided invaluable assistance to me in the preparation of this paper.

Much, but certainly not all, of the historic and current hostility toward lawyers derives, I believe, from the clash of values between the basic professional ethics . . . and common notions of morality and fairness. Against the background of these dilemmas . . . legal educators have been reluctant to enter the arena. My prediction is that they will continue to do so.[2]

Despite Schwartz's pessimism, emphasis on teaching legal ethics is increasing. Only 54 American law schools offered a course in legal ethics in 1958. Twenty years later, 133 (85 percent of United States law schools) required a course in professional ethics as a condition of graduation.[3] More important, there has been an extraordinary increase in the number of teachers in the area, and a growing body of law-review articles and teaching materials.[4] Whether this activity is a result of the ABA accreditation requirement, enacted in 1974, that law schools teach professional ethics,[5] or the high proportion of states in which professional ethics is a subject on the bar examination,[6] or the soul-searching of legal educators in the wake of the Watergate scandal,[7] there seems little doubt that the teaching of professional ethics has an accepted place in the basic curriculum of most American law schools, and that the literature on legal ethics is growing both in size and sophistication. A new *Journal of the Legal Profession* was founded in 1976; the Association of American Law Schools maintains a special section which presents programs at its annual meeting on the teaching of professional responsibility; the American Bar Association is hard at work, through a major special committee, revising the centerpiece of most courses and discussions of legal ethics, The Code of Professional Responsibility.

While formal course work and writing on the legal profession and its ethics may be a growth industry at present, the relationship between these developments and the troubling questions raised by Schwartz is fundamental to the subject of this paper. One recent exploration of these issues is Ronald M. Pipkins's analysis of an opinion survey of over 1,300 law students from seven diverse law schools during the 1975–76 school year. Pipkin concluded from the students' views that the ethics course in law school has "low esteem" in the curriculum hierarchy; it is perceived by students to be less valuable, to require less time and effort, and to be worse taught in comparison to most other law school courses. Pipkin suggests that present law school instruction in professional responsibility is not only failing, but that it may even be socializing students into believing that legal ethics is not important.[8] Pipkin's evidence contrasts sharply with a 1977 poll of legal ethics teachers who expressed no dissatisfaction with teaching the course or concern about student attitudes toward the course.[9]

This paper considers the issues raised by Schwartz and the special function and problems of the legal ethics course in terms of the development of American legal education. Section II presents a historical review of the efforts to graft the legal ethics course into the law curriculum and to create more effective means of teaching professional responsibility in the schools. Section III consists of comments on the place of legal ethics teaching in law schools today, and section IV reviews the kinds of materials commonly covered in these courses and the goals of these courses. Most courses devote substantial attention to The Code of Professional Responsibility, and accordingly, some of its problems are introduced in that section. Section V proposes a number of suggestions to improve legal ethics teaching in American law schools.

The thesis of this paper is that the structure of American legal education has created a difficult environment for a course which, of necessity, must focus on fundamental issues in the practice of law. The "activist critique," described in section IV, is an elaboration of the thesis that the design of American law schools has severely limited access to the actions and reasoning of practitioners and affected the selection and presentation of materials and the methods of inculcating professional ideals and values in students. The anomalous position of the legal ethics course in the law school curriculum mirrors the anomalous role of the schools in the profession. The teaching of professional ethics cannot be separated from the institutional role and mission of legal education.

II. A Brief History of Ethics in American Law Schools

The form of contemporary American legal education was created in the late nineteenth century when an entirely new method of classroom training in the university setting began to compete with the traditional law-office apprenticeship.[10] Usually attributed to Dean Christopher Columbus Langdell of Harvard Law School, this new book-oriented education carried three dominant (if sometimes only implicit) ethical assumptions.

First, law was conceived of as a science. The study of law required intense specialization and years of university study to introduce students to the fundamental rules of society. The principles of personal morality were presupposed. Fundamental concepts of right and wrong were beyond the scope or capabilities of the law schools; it was the more complex social morality embodied in the law that required exposition. The science of law was the handmaiden of a stable society: the lawyer was trained to learn and protect vested legal rights. The structure of legal education rested upon a concept of the moral order of which law was an instrument and expression.

Second, the new methods of studying law in the universities represented a powerful critique of the old ways of learning. The apprenticeship system taught craft, but not science. Implicit in the emergence of the new discipline of law was a downgrading of that training in the field which introduced students to the customs of practice. The professional "morality" learned in the law office was simply unworthy of study. Protocol and etiquette were not intellectual disciplines.

The founders of legal education assumed, therefore, that the cognitive and analytical study of law was, in important respects, concentrated on one aspect of a larger moral universe, whereas the morality of practice was so obvious (i.e., either trivial or basic) as to need no training.

The third ethical assumption was that the cognitive dimension of law study also had moral implications. Oliver Wendell Holmes described this in an 1886 oration before the Harvard Law School Association:

> I am not ready to say even that [what a law school does undertake to teach is law] without a qualification. It seems to me that nearly all the education which men can get from others is moral, not intellectual.[11]

Holmes believed that the great teacher should introduce students to the "profounder thought" and "subtiler joy" which changes their lives and renders them "incapable of mean ideals and easy self-satisfaction," ready to "live their lives more freely for the ferment"—the "inextinguishable fire"—imparted to them in law school.[12] In another famous lecture delivered to Harvard undergraduates in the same year, Holmes pointed to the heroic dimension of law study, as the student, in hope and despair, struggles to develop great thoughts amid the "black gulf of solitude."[13] This concept of education, as a form of initiation that disciplines the imagination, the sensibilities, and the mind, accepts the character-building role of learning. The function of the school, in this view, is to inculcate a morality of traits or dispositions, such as moral courage and conscientiousness, as natural by-products of the rigor of its intellectual or cognitive demands.[14]

Both the philosophy of Langdell and the special methodologies of Harvard legal education—limitation to postgraduate study, emphasis on the law library, the casebook as teaching material, and the "Socratic" classroom methodology—were competing in the late nineteenth century with the more prevalent modes of apprenticeship training and lecture forms of schooling. It was not until the first decades of the twentieth century that the Harvard model of legal education began to achieve the status of educational orthodoxy in law. During this period, the first modern professional organizations of lawyers began to form and cast about for methods of controlling a profession caught up in the pressures of industrial development, political turmoil, and the influx of immigrant attorneys. In 1887, the Alabama Bar Association adopted a Code of Ethics largely drawn from the work of two legal educators of the old school, George Sharswood's lectures at the University of Pennsylvania (*Legal Ethics,* 1854) and David Hoffman's "Fifty Resolutions in Regard to Professional Deportment" at the University of Maryland (*A Course of Legal Study,* 1836).[15]

The early Canons of Ethics were a mixed lot. They contained a number of different concepts—maxims of prudence or convention, manners, tactical advice, fraternalism, and idealism, as well as difficult normative issues, such as the loyalty and zeal owed the client "within the limits of the law" (Canon 10). The rapid growth of the Code movement appears to have coincided with a sense of siege upon the part of the leadership of the profession which was concerned about the increasing volley of attacks from outside, as well as about the large number of new attorneys who (in the words of the ABA ethics committee in 1906) had "no fixed ideals of ethical conduct," their fingers itching "in their eager quest for lucre."[16]

The first response of the schools to the Code movement was to commence lectures on the variety of subjects comprehended by the Codes. In 1898, the Ohio State University College of Law initiated a lecture course on ethics using as the text, Sharswood's *Legal Ethics*.[17] Maryland, in 1900, required a legal ethics course based on the "Code adopted by the Alabama and Virginia State Bar Association[s]."[18] Both Yale and the University of Chicago announced in 1902 a third-year lecture course on "Legal Ethics."[19] By 1915, the *American Law School Review* published a report indicating that 57 out of 81 law schools in the country (representing 75 percent of all law graduates) offered a course on legal ethics. The courses were usually lectures to senior students by judges or prominent attorneys. They ranged from four to fifteen hours, and used such texts as the Codes, or the Sharswood book, or the reports of the Committee on Professional Ethics of the New York County Lawyers' Association.[20]

The report also recounted the first presentation of the virtues of what has come to be known as the "pervasive method" of teaching legal ethics. Dean Thayer at Harvard reported no legal ethics course at that school, because of "incidental instructions" in the subject "throughout the student's course" and the fact that "we further call attention specifically to the American Bar Association's Canons by posting a large copy conspicuously in the hall of our main building and by distributing pamphlet copies to students."[21] The report concluded with a timeless truism: "There is a distinct movement among the law schools toward more instruction in professional ethics."[22]

Most legal ethics courses at the time of the *American Law School Review* report were both new and rudimentary. It is not surprising that a school like Harvard with a "modern" curriculum showed some disdain for old-fashioned ethics lectures. The subject was soon, however, to receive a "modern" treatment. In 1917, George P. Costigan, Jr., of Northwestern, published the first modern casebook on legal ethics which became the standard work in the field until the Cheatham casebook emerged in the late 1930s.

Costigan's *Cases on Legal Ethics* is a rich mixture of materials from early English reports, American and English cases, books of lawyers' reminiscences and biographies, as well as local bar and the American Bar Association Canons and the New York County Lawyers' Association "Questions and Answers" (i.e., opinions) by its Committee on Professional Ethics. The materials address descriptive and protocol matters such as the history and organization of the profession (contrasting the United States to the barrister-solicitor organization of the English bar), standards for admission to the bar, the grounds and procedures for discipline, the duties of lawyers to courts (e.g., abstaining from objectionable criticism, disclosing all relevant legal authorities), solicitation restrictions (prohibition against advertising and ambulance chasing), "pecuniary relations" (contingent and other fees, fee splitting, and so on) and appropriate trial conduct (treatment of other lawyers, lawyers as witnesses).

Costigan, however, had larger ambitions for his book: a substantial part of it was devoted to what he called "moral problems" such as Bentham's attack on the concept of confidentiality between lawyer and client, the problems of the attorney representing unjust causes, and the limits of advocacy for guilty criminal defendants. Many of these dilemmas are represented by historical stories and documents (largely from English sources) or biographical accounts of lawyers in famous cases.[23]

Costigan's collection of materials was designed, like the Codes and law school courses, as a surrogate in the schools for the loss of the supposed virtue of the older apprenticeship system: homogeneous socialization into the customs and dilemmas of practicing lawyers. Costigan himself in 1917 complained of the lack of serious attention paid to the subject in law schools. He characterized most of the lectures by outside practitioners as "general piffle" and described the "feelings of students that the faculty itself stigmatized the subject as relatively unimportant, both by allotting it such a brief time and by giving no credit for the work."[24]

Although the initial demands of the bar to make legal ethics a compulsory subject in law school predated the adoption of the Canons of Ethics in 1908,[25] by the mid- to late 1920s the pressure from the American Bar Association intensified. The ABA Committee on Professional Ethics and Grievances noted that while most schools had a course it consisted of two or three lectures a year at which attendance was small. The committee concluded that "the subject of professional ethics does not receive a sufficient place in the lawyer's scholastic education."[26] Despite resolutions by the ABA, for a number of years during the late 1920s, recommending compulsory study of ethics in the schools, the Association of American Law Schools strenuously opposed the requirement, fought a kind of delaying tactic by conducting a number of surveys of ethics teaching in the law schools, and succeeded in outlasting the ABA until the present requirement was eventually passed by the ABA during the summer of President Richard M. Nixon's resignation, in 1974.[27]

During the 1930s, the philosophical orientation of legal education was challenged in a manner that altered the nature of the debate about teaching legal ethics. The "formalism" of the late nineteenth century concept of the science of law had come under challenge from Holmes's ringing dissent against the reification in constitutional interpretation of "Mr. Herbert Spencer's Social Statics,"[28] and from Dean Roscoe Pound's "sociological jurisprudence." The progressives criticized the role lawyers played in the development of corporate empires. These developments were met, in part, by the attempt to affirm basic principles through promulgation of the Codes of Ethics. But by the late twenties the assumption that there existed commonly held moral values in society, fundamental to progressivism and its legal academic counterpart, sociological jurisprudence, had broken down. Legal Realism began its emergence.[29]

The Realist movement in American law schools was made up of an extremely diverse group of individuals, but it is possible to make some generalizations about their shared views on the responsibilities of lawyers, the role of legal educators, and the significance of the legal ethics course.

The Realists challenged the earlier assumptions about the scientific enterprise of learning law as either a subunit of the moral order of society or Pound's idea of law originating in some societal moral consensus or ethical system. To Realists, law no longer fit within a self-contained compartment in the hierarchy of rules about society and the world; the law performed a higher, integrative function as the guardian of the democratic process. Legal decisions inevitably had moral dimensions because the law in a democratic system was the chief means we employ to affect public policy. Learning the law was therefore an interdisciplinary exercise that involved surveying the political, economic, and social consequences of legal rules and procedures.

[W]e either integrate [wrote Karl Llewelyn] the background of social and economic fact and policy, course by course, or fail at our job . . . I do not refer to "teaching Legal Ethics" in a course. I refer to the setting up of every course to bear, *inter alia,* on what the job in society of that branch of law may really be, and on how well the job is being performed.[30]

The function of law school, in the Realist view, was to impart to students certain sensitivities to the consequences of legal decisions. The law school's mission involved a much more self-conscious acceptance of the importance of inculcating values than the early founders conceived for the scientific study of the law. The mission of the school was to impart high ethical ideals in terms of assessing the effects of law from a perspective informed by reference to sister disciplines, which provide "the wherewithal to weigh [the facts] and their implications for a People."[31]

The Realist concept of lawyers as the philosopher-princes of democratic society was largely focused on the attorney as policymaker and legislator, not on the narrower categories of lawyer-client decisions which were important to the Canons-oriented traditional ethics courses. Accordingly, the Realists, like many of their predecessors, professed disdain for such ethics courses when true ethical inquiry (focusing on critical examination of the defects and untoward impacts of the law) ought to pervade *all* law school courses.

One leading Realist, Jerome Frank, was in general more skeptical than many of his colleagues of the policymaking functions of lawyers and more concerned to define the special province of the lawyer as the guardian of justice, particularly in terms of the operation of courts. Frank wrote that lawyers have a "special moral duty to assure their clients a fair trial, they do *not* have a social duty to create a scientifically based "heaven-on-earth." He was no less concerned with the law reform mission of the schools; he preferred that they focus on the "idea of equality before the law" and the frustrations of that ideal in the day-to-day reality (the "blight") of the court system.[32] Frank's concern with the lawyer's relationship to his client and the institutional relationship of lawyers to the court system led him to suggest a methodological reform in legal education—the practice of law by students in university-related clinics.[33] Frank's idea drew some attention and criticism, but the clinical idea gained little headway until the late 1960s. Discussion of clinics as a vehicle for teaching ethics was minimal.

Despite the antipathy of many academics toward the separate ethics course and the rather desultory lecturer-from-the-bar methods often used to communicate the course materials to students, some change began to occur in the subject matter of the legal ethics course, largely under the influence of the Realists. Elliot Cheatham, in a 1932 address before the Association of American Law Schools, called for the schools to initiate the study of the profession of law in terms of "the needs of effective law administration."[34]

Cheatham described a new approach to the teaching of ethics in law schools, which he contrasted to other approaches such as the "adherence to the genteel tradition" (or general moral tone of the school) and the "dogmatic method" (or traditional course on the Code). Cheatham's proposed course on the profession of law added substantially to the traditional subject matter in legal ethics by attempting to examine the bar and the bench *as institutions,* capable of improving standards for the administration of justice. This was classic Realism: members of the bar, in fact, form a collective body which has enormous impact on legal institutions; students should be introduced to a critical perspective on the power and potential of the organized bar as agents of obstruction or instruments of desirable social change. The rhetorical high-water mark of this idea was an address by Dean Clark of Yale, in 1935, in which he summoned the law schools "to turn from their success among the precedents to assist in the endeavor to build a better bar. It is a much more difficult task; it calls for what Dean Pound used to like to call "social engineering" of a high and original kind."[35]

There had long been a tradition in the ethical literature of emphasizing the public nature of the legal profession. Early nineteenth-century legal moralists like Sharswood viewed the lawyer as akin to an agent for the divine lawgiver whose task was "to maintain the ancient land marks, to respect authority, to guard the integrity of law as a science, that it may be a certain rule of decision, and promote that security of life, liberty and property, which . . . is the greatest end of human society and government."[36] The Realists accepted the high pretension of this role, shorn of the religious and moral structure that justified it. They sought, therefore, to replace ethics with what they termed a "professional ethic" designed to inculcate values, and a conception of "the law as a public profession charged with inescapable social responsibilities."[37]

> If the law is to remain what it has been [wrote Sidney Simpson], a profession, some means must be provided for instilling into these same journeymen that sense of obligation and responsibility which is of the essence of a profession. . . . When legal education is committed to academic institutions, the problem is much more difficult. It is a problem in moral education . . . . Preaching is of no avail. Formal teaching of "legal ethics" tends to become instruction either in legal etiquette or in how far a lawyer may safely go, the former relatively unimportant and the latter actively pernicious.[38]

Simpson went on to argue it was not enough to transmit the past and present traditions of the bar because these traditions are for the most part unethical, narrow, and selfish (citing the lack of legal services for the poor and the proliferation of lawyers for business and financial interests with no thought of the public consequences). The solution lay largely in the development of a personal commitment or academic professional ethic reminiscent of Holmes's articulation of the study of law as moral education:

> Education in responsibility must be largely, indirect and more by example than by precept . . . . To be effective, it must pervade every course and every aspect of the school's life . . . . It follows that education for wise discharge of the public responsibilities of the legal profession is a problem for each individual teacher of law . . . . Certainly it cannot be solved by "platitudinous exhortation," or by requiring exposure to courses in "legal ethics," or by compelling every student to take part in a legal aid "clinic." [S]uch education must proceed pervasively in each teacher's instruction and in his relations with his students.[39]

Even Lon Fuller, who by his own proclamation was not a Realist, viewed as an important function of the schools to "inculcate" a proper sense of professional responsibility toward client and public.[40] In fact, although Realism probably did not become an important orientation in law schools until the postwar years, Realist views on legal ethics in the 1930s were widely shared by Realists and non-Realists alike. The scholarly writing of the 1930s and 1940s was responding to the same set of cultural facts: the dramatic increase in legislation, a turn-of-the-century faith in man's ability to solve the world's problems, the rise of great business and financial interests and the predictable rush of lawyers to profit personally by "serving" wealthy clients at the expense of the profession's ideal of public service, the unmet legal needs of the "other than wealthy" members of society, the new-found respectability of utilitarianism as a theory of the source of ethical duty, and the felt threat to democratic values in the thirties, forties, and fifties. To a great extent, these cultural influences nullified jurisprudential differences between the theoreticians. Regardless of one's definition of law, a moral crisis in the profession was a shared problem demanding cooperative solutions.

Everyone agreed that it was the job of the schools at least to attempt to impress students with a "sense of moral responsibility." Everyone also agreed that this goal was difficult to accomplish and that the straightforward preaching of moral precepts was ineffective. Debate over teaching method was neither extensive nor heated. Legal ethics courses, when mentioned in the writings at all, were generally disparaged as boring, tedious, and insufficient. The pervasive approach, whereby each teacher had the duty of conveying the meaning of at least some sense of morality or ethical standards, was overwhelmingly preferred.

After the disruption of the war years and staggering postwar enrollment increases, the Association of American Law Schools and the Council of the Section of Legal Education of the ABA began, in the early 1950s, to explore the implications of the Realist consensus. The question was "how important lawyers are and how much more they could contribute to the national life if they possessed a greater awareness of the public responsibilities that attach to their positions as lawyers."[41] After an unsuccessful effort by the Association of American Law Schools (AALS) and ABA to fund a study on value identification and transmission, a committee of the AALS sponsored a conference at Boulder, Colorado, in 1956 (Boulder I), to discuss the problem of educating law students in their public responsibilities as lawyers.

The Boulder I attendees were highly diversified in terms of schools, geography, legal and philosophical perspectives. Consequently, they failed to agree on which core societal values underlay the concept of public responsibility. There was some agreement in their critique of legal education: the "ethically sterilizing" effect of appellate case-method pedagogy; the overriding law school goal of wanting students to learn how to use law "with scant regard to ethics and morals"; the "sprawling," diversified curriculum tending toward specialty competence, not responsibility training.[42] The participants' remedies and prescriptions for change in terms of the morality which should be taught in law school included inculcation of natural law philosophies, espousal of social and legal activism, Lon Fuller's "inner morality" of law through dedication to the forms of social order recognizing the "difficulties in any exposition of the moral system," dedication to human dignity, and doing nothing.[43]

Specific suggestions were equally diverse. The conference explored such structural changes as altering the selection of law school recruits, and curriculum supplements, such as more active student bar associations and extensive practitioner involvement. In its curriculum proposals, the conference strongly supported the so-called pervasive method, that is, having throughout the curriculum:

> incidental comment on ethical considerations within the regular courses, bringing out the ethical presuppositions in the discussion of the cases, the private and public implications of the handling of the cases, and the points at which ethical judgment enters into the interpretation of the law.[44]

But there was also widespread agreement on the validity of concentrated courses, whether they be traditional (nonlaw) ethical theory courses, a professional ethics course (subject matter not well defined except in relation to Cheatham's casebook), or simply courses in jurisprudence, comparative law, and international law, or internships and "role-taking" involving some conscious ethical component.[45] The final result of the conference was a call for encouragement of experimentation in developing more effective means to improve awareness in students and lawyers of their public responsibilities as practitioners and citizens.[46]

In the wake of the Boulder Conference, the AALS committee undertook yet another survey of ethics teaching. Of the 85 AALS schools replying, 54 (or 64 percent) indicated the presence of a specific course on the subject, usually a one-semester-hour course required of seniors (often ungraded or pass-fail). The extent of pervasive teaching appeared to be minimal; only 36 courses were identified as involving instructors who introduced ethical issues and values into their teaching subject. The subject matter taught in the required ethics courses was described by the committee as including the Canons of Professional Ethics; the nature of the profession; law practice matters such as acquiring a practice, solicitation of clients, and advertising; "the lawyer's duty of competence, good faith, honesty and integrity and his relation to his client, in terms of comparative independence or subordination" [presumably of the lawyer, not the client]; matters of conduct in court and relations with other lawyers; fees; and preventing unauthorized practice.[47]

Another activity begun in the early 1950s, the Joint Conference on Professional Responsibility of the ABA and AALS, issued a Report in 1958 which was not only the best, but perhaps the only attempt to articulate the philosophical premises and reasoning behind the Canons of Professional Ethics. The stress, as with Boulder I, was on the public role of the lawyer as advocate and counselor, designer of collaborative frameworks, and private practitioner or citizen. The Joint Conference Report, largely the work of Professor Lon Fuller of Harvard Law School,[48] undertook to provide a philosophical rationale for the adversary system and the public benefits of serving private interests, provided the lawyer's ultimate loyalty ran to "procedures and institutions" in his or her role as trustee "for the integrity of those fundamental processes of government and self-government upon which the successful functioning of our society depends."[49]

After the theoretical explorations of Boulder I and Joint Conference Report of 1959, the emphasis of thinking in law school circles began to center on the pedagogical problem of getting the "professional responsibility" message across, rather than on a theoretical concern with the nature of the problem. This shift of emphasis is revealed by a comparison of Boulder I and a subsequent conference held in 1968 (Boulder II). At Boulder I approximately twenty-five participants tried to define what constitutes a lawyer's professional duties. No such attempt was made at Boulder II. Boulder II (sponsored by the AALS and a Ford Foundation-funded Council on Education in Professional Responsibility) involved over a hundred participants and accepted as broad a definition as possible of what constitutes a lawyer's professional responsibilities. The Boulder II conferees were willing to accept the approaches debated at Boulder I without attempting to resolve contradictions among them. The conference was, as a result, more fragmented and less interesting dialectically than its predecessor. The exchange of ideas was not as sharp or stimulating, but more pedagogically developed ideas were articulated, simply because no asserted theoretical premise was challenged or scrutinized. Boulder II was a cooperative endeavor with several approaches to legal-ethical problems explored, and the participants felt no need to arrive at a synthesis or resolution.[50]

This pluralistic approach to the teaching of "professional responsibilities" is characteristic of most recent writings. The authors are not so concerned with convincing the reader of what professional duties are as with deciding how they can be effectively taught. The debate that surfaced at Boulder I—whether a lawyer has a duty to his client or society, or to the improvement of the substantive law or the reform of procedural law (attention to Fuller's "forms" or "fundamental processes of government"), higher ethical ideals or individual integrity—has been resolved in the simplest, consensual way: a lawyer's professional responsibility embraces *all* of these duties.

One major new theme that had already surfaced at the time of Boulder II was the role of controlled practice or clinical experience in the teaching of ethics. The earliest justification for the legal clinic was its potential for promoting professional competence.[51] During the thirties, the idea of clinics began to receive systematic attention as a possible purveyor of "legal ethics." J. Bradway noted the capacity of the clinic for providing training in legal ethics and public service.[52] Jerome Frank referred to the "ethics" dimension of legal clinics in an 1933 article: "Professional ethics can be effectively taught only if the students while learning the canon of ethics have available some first-hand observation of the ways in which the ethical problems of the lawyer arise and of the actual habits (the 'mores') of the bar."[53] Some other writers cited the clinic as a medium through which "legal ethics" can be taught, both in terms of public or "social responsibility," and "private professionalism."[54]

At Boulder II it was agreed generally that legal clinics were useful as a medium for teaching all aspects of professional responsibility. The main focus of the clinical movement at this time, however, was on the legal needs, first raised in the 1930s, of the "other than wealthy." This service aspect of professionalism, it was argued, should be communicated by assisting the student, both as an individual and as a part of the profession, to feel a sense of obligation to the courts, public, and society in varying ways. The clinical experience could impress upon the student involved with the local community that law was a service profession and not a business. The student was supposed to assimilate the idea of the lawyer and the law as a general "guardian" of society's legal rights. In as heavily a legalistic society as ours, the lawyer's role necessarily embraced reform of the law, substantively and procedurally, and an active reaching out to those members of the public who otherwise would not enjoy its protection.

Some writers and participants at Boulder II did not try to disguise the fact that one of the main, if not *the* main, virtues of the clinical program is its capacity for bringing the student face to face with the failures and inadequacies of the legal system, adversary ethics, and the mechanisms by which we administer legal services. This point of view was expressed most openly by Jerome Carlin:

> [T]he object of the game is not the education of students. Our clinical programs are not designed merely to instill professional responsibility in the student, nor to teach him better, and they should not be. We should have such programs in order to discharge the public responsibility of the law schools. The law schools ought to be places of service in the community. They ought to be places that are shaping the future for the community. Clinical programs . . . are instruments of social action for social change and vehicles for the radical restructuring of society.[55]

The clinical movement led to a more radical criticism of the "ethos" of legal education and the exploration of the ethical implications of the student-teacher relationship in law school. Although the 1960s gave birth to a foundation (the Council for Legal Education in Professional Responsibility—CLEPR) committed to funding clinical programs and changing legal education "from the top" to make a more socially responsive law school,[56] it also generated criticism of legal education's moral neutrality, its antihumanitarianism, its espousal of an adversary ethic antithetical to individual moral integrity, and its total detachment from aspects of human and professional development, such as emotional sensitivity. The law school classroom was cast as the chief culprit: it was viewed as dehumanizing, if not sadistic, destructive of values (other than intense skepticism), and a tactic for promoting hostility and competition among students. The efficiency of the Socratic method and the resulting institutional structure of most law schools (i.e., extremely high faculty-student ratios compared to other graduate and professional schools) was felt to preclude systematic contact between faculty and students outside the aggressive and highly authoritarian environment of the classroom. Law school, according to these critics, fostered in students a dangerous and demeaning division between thought and feeling; student self-esteem was ignored or challenged in the process of legal education.[57] A number of reforms were suggested and adopted, ranging from modification of severe grading procedures to the development of courses in such vital skills as interviewing and counseling. A variety of other suggestions were made by psychiatrists such as Alan Stone and Andrew Watson—fostering teaching environments requiring cooperation among students, more self-conscious display by teachers of their ideological positions,[58] human relations training for teachers and students, better advisement programs, and effective use of clinical training.[59]

Gary Bellow, in an important contribution to a national conference sponsored by CLEPR in 1973, described the "central feature of the clinical method as its conscious use, both conceptually and operationally, of the dynamics of role adjustment in social life." Students in a practice setting need to deal with the anxiety generated by an unfamiliar environment and to justify their conduct. "The knowledge and motivational consequences of role adjustment" create a more reciprocal setting in which students can legitimately question their teachers. Thus, clinics "offer the possibility of redressing the balance of authority in the present teacher-student relationship in the direction of greater student-initiated speculation, criticism and thought."[60]

According to Bellow, the student's acting *in the lawyer's role,* can open up a student's resistance to self-reflection and improve his understanding of the legal system. The often random and unstructured nature of practice, because of its very intensity and psychological importance to the student, establishes tensions in the learning process. "One of the reasons clinical education offers so much promise for teaching professional responsibility is that students are implicated in the outcome of choice. Moral discourse is not merely a discussion of possibilities, but a framework for justification and evaluation of concrete action."[61] The demands on teachers are extraordinary, not only because they must intervene to protect clients and others, but they must also help students generalize from their activities in order to structure the experience. The integration required in the clinic between theory and practice, classroom subjects and other bodies of thought or experience, and choice and judgment is unique in the law school setting. Clinics, therefore, are concerned with professional responsibility in a way not possible in classroom-dominated education. The clinic student is "implicated in some of the choices which are the subject of inquiry. He or she must live with consequences in a way which makes discussion of the problem of responsibility a meaningful concern."[62] Under this view, clinics challenge the original isolation of theory and practice in law schools as a method of resolving conflicts of professional education in a university setting. The structure of legal education, the educational theory behind law schools, and the "paper chase" itself become ethical issues highlighted and, to an important extent, addressed by the clinical experience.

The impetus of clinical programs in the late 1960s—community service and social change—shifted during the 1970s as former legal services attorneys teaching in law school clinics confronted the politics of the 1970s, including the politics of tenure. The ambitions of clinicians, when not focused on skills or performance training, took a more pedagogical orientation: clinics could leaven general law school teaching methods through the introduction of techniques like simulation and video playback criticism of student performance, or they could pursue Bellow's psychologizing of legal ethics by using performance in the lawyer's role as a vehicle for exploring the contours of the attorney-client relationship.

The most recent development in the field of teaching ethics in law school is the expression of interest by philosophers in the possibilities of linking traditional ethical studies and legal ethics. A 1977 summer "Institute on Law and Ethics" and follow-up conference in 1979 sponsored by the Council for Philosophical Studies explored the issue described by Bellow in 1973:

> The problem of engaging students in discussions of the norms of professional and private conduct and their relationship is an extremely complex and difficult one. Students, in general, come to such discussions with considerable suspicion and, at least, a verbal commitment to a radical relativism. The problems of generalizing a common base of agreement from which attempts to draw distinctions and incremental judgments can be made are considerable. It is complicated by the absence, to my knowledge, of any writing on professional responsibility that adequately draws on the philosophic[al] literature of ethics, values, or obligations.[63]

The Conference Report made a number of recommendations for improving law school ethics courses and undergraduate courses in ethics, legal process, and the philosophy of law; and suggested, as did Boulder I, the need for more experimentation in terms of collaboration between legal educators and moral philosophers.[64]

III. The Teaching of Ethics—1979

Virtually every theme raised during the past hundred years now finds expression in the diverse attitudes of legal educators and members of the bar toward the "subject" of ethics in law schools.[65] To an important extent the term "ethics" is a misnomer, for the subject (usually titled "professional responsibility or "the legal profession") is much different in scope from ethics in any traditional sense of that term. It comprehends professional etiquette, the organization of the profession, aspects of practice management, as well as the law of practice embodied in The Code of Professional Responsibility and case law, including that of malpractice. Moreover, concepts of ethics in law school transcend even the idea of a specific subject matter.

Many legal educators still view legal education as "moral education" in terms not dissimilar to that conceived by Holmes almost a century ago. Judge Jack Weinstein, for example, speaks of "students absorbing, from the day they enter law school, a sense of what the functions of the profession are and what their individual role is to be in that profession" through a subtle process of absorbing the attitudes of their professors and peers. What is essential is a "committed faculty," writes Weinstein, "engaged in severe and challenging intellectual work . . . teaching by . . . attitudes the importance of strict and honest intellectual standards . . . inspiring their students by their own ethical positions."[66] To the traditional view, hailing the emotional discipline and high moral value of rigorous intellectual work, is added the Realist focus on the lawyer as a society leader and reformer, the *noblesse oblige* of "an exalted profession."[67] The best teachers adopt a critical attitude toward law—both substantive doctrine and the delivery structure of legal services—together with analysis of reform alternatives which are morally less objectionable than existing structures. What teachers do *is* ethics. There is in law a double legacy: the moral pretension of the intellectual about character building through rigorous cognitive work, together with the "chutzpah" of the Realists about law as the ultimate school of public policy studies. On the other hand, law teachers do not teach ethics *openly*. Felix Frankfurter commented on his law training that "There weren't any courses on ethics, but the place was permeated by ethical presuppositions and assumptions and standards. On the whole, to this day I am rather leery of explicit ethical instruction."[68] Costigan, writing in 1917, commented that his fellow teachers found the words "legal ethics" so objectionable that they would happily "vote to abolish the words altogether."[69] Ethics viewed as criticism of the law and the structure and practices of the profession is, by and large, championed by legal educators.

While law schools are not embarrassed to espouse the morality of inculcating personal virtues that arise from difficult intellectual work, and to acknowledge their role as critics of our system of justice, there has been a persistent theme of disdain in some quarters for the type of legal ethics the bar has wanted taught—instruction on the Code, the disciplinary structure, and the like. Many legal educators follow the Realists by viewing these matters as intellectually and morally sterile. Part of this tension between bar and academe arises no doubt from the peculiar structure of American legal education, that is, the rather rigid demarcation that separates schooling and practice, and the exceptionally "narrow definition," in Willard Hurst's phrase, of legal education itself. Law schools have, by and large, refused to expand the basic limits originally set by Langdell, except for the enormous post-World War II growth in the elective curriculum, largely in specialty subjects and some interdisciplinary studies. The clinical component in legal education, despite the liberal application of Ford Foundation funding through CLEPR, does not enjoy a significant or central place in most law schools. The anomaly of legal education, mentioned in the introduction to this paper, is that law schools do not pretend to produce fully competent practitioners, although they now enjoy a virtual monopoly of the initial training to become a lawyer.[70] The persistent pressure by the organized bar to teach "legal ethics" in law school comes from its own endorsement of law school as the exclusive method of entry to the profession and the failure of the bar to address the problem of systematic or uniform instruction to new entrants in the disciplinary system, customs, and manners of the profession.

The course on legal ethics has usually been at the center of the debate.[71] Tied to the belief of many law teachers that the content of "ethics" is somehow uninteresting or unworthy of fine minds[72] is a set of assumptions about the uselessness of preaching or "exhortation" as a pedagogical device,[73] and a belief that student values are so thoroughly ingrained that they cannot be affected by law school. The response to this position comes from two quarters. The most recent attack comes from the psychiatrist Andrew Watson who uses a tactic peculiar to his trade:

> [P]rofessionalism is psychologically threatening to law professors because they have had little or no experience in dealing with these matters, nor have they resolved the personal problems that facilitate professional behavior. Never having suffered these conflicts directly, they cannot help those who are struggling with them. Nor can they freely empathize with such suffering, since this would subject them to a source of anxiety that they quite naturally attempt to avoid. The end result is to make law faculties quite unmotivated to move into these areas of education.[74]

Another attack focuses on the assumption that the teaching of legal ethics is meant to uplift the completed moral personality of the postgraduate student. Dean Kinnane of Wyoming in an article in the early 1930s stated the argument in favor of teaching ethics in law school in direct terms. First, much of what is needed to be taught is not ethics in any traditional sense, but is information about the contingencies of professional decorum, the disciplinary structure, and the conventions of the bar, which must somehow be provided to students as long as the professional schools conceive of their role as separate from practice. To neglect such instruction is to provide a trap for the unwary new lawyer whose common sense or moral training might not alert him to some of the rules of the fraternity relating to "a matter on which the experts became agreed only a year ago."[75]

Kinnane's second argument is that the "morality" taught in the separate ethics course is not the easy stuff of avoiding embezzlement of a client's funds "where the moral path is clear." Nor is legal ethics a series of corollaries or derivations from "ordinary morality," but a special morality which poses unusual dilemmas requiring some analytical training or viewpoint. These are matters concerning which the profession has been, and is, "in doubt," e.g., "just how the principle that the lawyer owes the utmost fidelity to the interests of his clients is controlled by the principle that he is also an officer of the court . . . "[76]

Ethics viewed in Kinnane's terms as analysis of the role dilemmas and problems of lawyers faced with conflicting professional values faces a difficult terrain in American law schools. The diagnosis by Murray Schwartz, cited earlier, is probably an accurate description of the general ethos of law schools. The schools are affected by a high degree of specialization in the profession, reflected in the interests and offerings of faculty in the curriculum; a general (but by no means universal) disinterest on the part of faculty in "practice" issues such as a lawyer's obligations to the client; and the limited role in most schools of clinical training in the curriculum as a whole, or in stimulating the kind of reflective ethical component in student practice advocated by clinical theorists like Bellow.

Suggesting, as does Schwartz, that law school is an "inhospitable" place to undertake, on any systematic scale, exploration of the moral development of future lawyers does not mean law faculties are institutionally hostile to the basic course or teachers of the course. Indeed, Schwartz's diagnosis may explain the enthusiasm with which the course is seized upon as a means of avoiding an extraordinarily difficult set of problems. Almost all American law schools have a course on legal ethics, professional responsibility, or the legal profession, and usually it is required for graduation. Although the course is now generally accepted as a part of the curriculum of American law schools, it is probably fair to say the subject is viewed by both faculty and students as being somewhat peripheral to the curriculum compared to the role of torts, contracts, property, taxation, or even less central courses such as antitrust. It is usually—although there are significant exceptions—a third-year offering with the reputation as a "gut," or easy subject, taught in large sections of about 60 to 150 students meeting one or two hours a week for one semester. Advanced courses or seminars are extremely rare.[77]

The 1975-76 survey by Ronald Pipkin, cited earlier, concluding that the course is held in low regard by students, would receive a mixed reception among teachers of the course today. Fifty legal ethics teachers from a wide variety of law schools responded to my letter of inquiry sent to a list of about three hundred active professional responsibility teachers. Many correspondents, in effect, confirm Pipkin's conclusions by citing the low level of student work, and attitudes of hostility or condescension or resistance. On the other hand, a significant number felt that student attitude was improving, or that their course altered the initial skepticism students bring to the subject. A high proportion of correspondents asserted that although other law faculty either accepted (i.e., tolerated) or approved the course, very few of the faculty wished to teach it. This view corresponds to the figures from the 1977 Detroit Conference survey indicating that about three-fourths of faculty of all ranks who taught the professional responsibility course had five years or less experience in the subject area, and most of these had been teaching it two years or less.[78] The relatively high frequency of inexperienced hands suggests that the course, like the queen of spades, may be passed around among the faculty with some degree of regularity, and could be construed as some support for Pipkin's conclusion that, at least at a number of schools, the course is poorly taught.

One of the pedagogical initiatives sponsored in the midsixties—the "problem method" of instruction in legal ethics—has grown to become the dominant classroom pedagogy of the late 1970s.[79] These texts and courses are organized around situations or problems that are often written in rich factual detail as a means of piquing student interest and discussion about practice decisions faced by attorneys. The advantages of this method are the coverage of issues for which court cases or the written literature do not provide a sharp focus, and the engagement of students in the actual use of the Code to solve problems whereby they may assess its (in)effectiveness.[80] The pedagogical risks with the problem method—unless the class is carefully handled—are that repetitive use of difficult problems may create a sense of conceptual incoherence and breed a thoroughgoing relativism among those subjected to a strict diet of dilemmas. Casebooks are still popular among a number of teachers, and despite the total disrepute in which the lecture method stands in the law school world, almost half of the law schools surveyed in 1977 reported lecturing as a mode of instruction in the subject in their school.[81]

Some other generalizations can be drawn from our thoroughly unscientific survey and correspondence with legal ethics teachers. Most (not all) teachers felt that the output and quality of textbooks and scholarly writing were improving; and that interest in the field was rising. One of the most interesting findings in the 1977 Detroit Conference survey was the fact that many teachers (representing over one-third of the 156 schools responding to the survey) used their own materials rather than one of the many text and casebooks now on the market.[82] The tradition of the cottage industry in home-grown course materials is still strong despite the acknowledged quality of the published course materials. Indeed, there are a number of experimental efforts, including the use of a computer exercise on the Code to free classroom time for discussion, the use of role-playing exercises, team-teaching with philosophers or individuals trained in social ethics, and the conscious pedagogical use of Laurence Kohlberg's moral development theories.[83] While there may not be any special attractiveness to legal ethics in the intellectual pecking order of legal education, healthy signs exist of dissatisfaction, renewed scholarly and pedagogical interest, and attempts to improve classroom materials and their presentation.

IV. The Goals and Materials of the Ethics Course

A. Subject Goals

Concepts of legal ethics or professional responsibility are extraordinarily varied. Some teachers focus on drilling their students on the Code. Others accept a more expansive notion of the law of lawyer conduct, but deliberately limit their materials and discussion to statutory, administrative, and case law. Still others are primarily interested in the moral dilemmas of practitioners that are not necessarily covered by legal rules or principles. Some teachers focus on the formal and informal structure of the governance and regulation of the legal profession as an entity in much the same way a teacher of Communications Law or Public Utilities Law would address a regulated enterprise. Many teachers attempt to do a little of everything within the confines (typically) of two semester hours, thus requiring a high degree of selectivity of materials, even from commonly used casebooks, many of which are substantial enough to be used for four-credit-hour courses. As we have mentioned earlier, a large number of faculty ignore the publishers and create their own materials. While it is perilous to attempt to generalize about a "typical" ethics course, there are a number of commonly accepted areas of analysis.

1. The Code of Professional Responsibility

Virtually all courses must deal in some way with the Code of Professional Responsibility, if only, as one teacher noted, to castigate it as a disgrace to a learned profession. The Code is a statute (or court rule with statutory effect), regulating the behavior of lawyers, which is an important part of the practice of law. Its provisions, ambiguities, and purposes or framework require exposition. The complexities of the statute need to be interpreted. Most teachers of the subject, therefore, seek in one form or another to acquaint students with the Code provisions and highlight some of the problems which the Code does not resolve. It may therefore be helpful to review briefly the "ethics" of the ABA Code.

The Code, made effective in 1970, is, to a large extent, a redrafting and restructuring of the Canons of Professional Ethics (1908), and thus it contains a wide range of utterly disparate material—norms of etiquette, inspiration, obligation, and law-practice economics and organization—assembled within a topical framework that suggests these are of relatively equal significance. The important innovative feature of the Code over the Canons was designed as a response to the obvious decline, during the sixty years of experience with the Canons, of what Geoffrey Hazard describes as the informal "mechanisms of fraternal control by the profession at large and of community control through individual reputation," which were the chief methods of enforcement of the published ethical precepts. What was clearly needed was a "body of law" or regulatory system.[84]

The Code preserves the spirit of the old Canons, and creates better enforcement standards through a two-tiered document. Under nine general categories, called canons or "axiomatic norms," the lawyer is first presented with ethical considerations (ECs) that are "aspirational in character" and then with disciplinary rules (DRs) or minimum standards of conduct, violation of which subjects a lawyer to disciplinary action. While this distinction between standards of excellence and standards of minimal performance sensibly attempts to provide both vision and clearly articulated rules of conduct, the distinction is neither systematically followed nor is it as helpful or clear a differentiation as the drafters of the Code intended.[85] The ECs sometimes appear to be broadly drafted guidelines, appropriate for less rigid and informal regulation, in contrast to the more determinate rules and rigid imperatives of the DRs. The ECs may address the more situational and hard-to-codify domains of conduct, where "qualities like affection, integrity, imagination, sympathy, and judgment are the primary desiderata," as opposed to the hard-and-fast DRs. Or the ECs may simply be those matters which, unlike DR subjects, are not susceptible of enforcement.[86] The allocation between the two kinds of norms was made in the context of a desire to incorporate the tradition of the Canons in a more modern framework and the realization that the disciplinary machinery—exposed in 1970 by the scathingly critical "Clark Committee" of the ABA—[87] was largely inadequate to the task of enforcement.

The ECs and DRs are elaborately footnoted with citations to court decisions, books, articles, and the enormous body of interpretative literature embodied in the formal opinions and "informal" opinions (i.e., those applicable to narrower topics of less importance) of the ABA, state, and local bar association ethics committees. The ABA Code has been enacted almost verbatim by court rules or legislation in most of the states. It is the statutory standard of conduct in state systems for disciplining members of the bar (which have much improved in the wake of the Clark Committee), and it is the most authoritative text to guide court decisions and the thousands of advisory opinions issued annually by law firms and official bodies in response to attorneys' inquiries relating to "ethical" problems.

The Code, as we have indicated, is a potpourri of values. As a guild document it regulates competition among lawyers and between lawyers and nonlawyers, enunciating, for example, prohibitions against certain forms of advertising (DR 2–101); accepting a client unless the client's other counsel approves or withdraws (EC 2–30); referral or finder's fees (DR 2–107); aiding the "unauthorized" practice of law by nonlawyers (DR 3–101 [A]); and sharing fees with a nonlawyer (DR 3–102).

Together with these "fraternal" measures are a number of items designed to address problems in the public perception of the bar and the court by regulating matters affecting the appearance of impropriety and wrongful conduct, such as proscribing commingling a client's funds with the lawyers' (DR 9–102); making false accusations against a judge (DR 8–102[B]) tampering with jurors (DR 7–108); serving as both counsel and witness in a case (DR 5–102); and getting too closely involved in business with a client (DR 5–103 and DR 5–104).

The Code also serves as the written surrogate for a wise counselor. It is a repository of maxims ranging from tactical advice to high principle. The Code enjoins lawyers to be temperate and dignified (EC 1–5, EC 7–36); refrain from morally reprehensible conduct (EC 1–5); represent clients or causes unpopular in the community (EC 2–27); take pride in their work (EC 6–5); refrain from haranguing and offensive tactics (EC 7–37); and be punctual and courteous and follow local customs (EC 7–38).

Thus far we have been discussing aspects of lawyer's conduct regulated by the Code that do not rise to the level of issues of personal morality. Among the most controversial portions of the Code are the provisions that address the special moral problems of lawyers.

2. Role Morality

In practice, a lawyer's moral principles (most lawyers would argue) must on many occasions be different from those of ordinary persons because a lawyer owes a special fealty to the client. Murray Schwartz describes this role morality in terms of two "principles" that define the nature of the special moral obligation and the status of the attorney acting as advocate:

The Principle of Professionalism for the Advocate	"When acting as an advocate, a lawyer must, within the established constraints upon professional behavior, maximize the likelihood that the client will prevail."
The Principle of Nonaccountability for the Advocate	"When acting as an advocate for a client according to the Principle of Professionalism, a lawyer is neither legally, professionally, nor morally accountable for the means used or the ends achieved."[88]

Specifically, the attorney has three nonordinary (or professional) obligations: (1) zeal for the cleint's interests, deriving from the lawyer's unique obligation to speak, act, and "make the case" for his client;[89] (2) the duty to exercise independent judgment for a client; and (3) the duty to preserve clients' confidences. The Code makes these obligations explicit. Much less clear are their limits when they clash with other values, particularly the duty of the lawyer to uphold the law and the integrity of the court system and to avoid conduct involving dishonesty, deceit, or misrepresentation.

(a) Zeal

The Code spells out a number of limits to the general injunction to represent a client zealously, such as prohibiting the use of false evidence, or the filing of law suits merely to injure another party.[90] Geoffrey Hazard describes how narrowly drawn these limits are: most refer to conduct in litigation, such as "lawyer misbehavior that affects other lawyers" which can be counteracted or diffused by the presence of other lawyers and the judge; the proscribed acts, including lies, have "little or no greater breadth than that imposed" under the law of fraud;[91] and ABA opinions[92] and court rules[93] have significantly limited the extent to which a lawyer is required to reveal client fraud or perjury.

(b) Independent Judgment

The Code enjoins a lawyer from accepting or continuing in a case, absent consent, where the exercise of independent judgment will be affected by representation of another client and when it is likely to involve the attorney in representing "differing interests."[94] While the ECs give some examples of typical "conflict of interest" situations, such as husband and wife in a divorce or codefendants in a criminal case,[95] the range of problems generated by these provisions—which are often cited by lawyers as the most common set of ethical issues faced in practice—is enormous. A variety of ancillary issues arise, including the problem of representing clients whose interests differ, but at different times, and the issue of vicarious disqualification of a partner or associate of a lawyer disqualified because of conflict of interest.[96] Much of the elaboration of doctrine in this field has been litigated and is susceptible to traditional casebook exposition and analysis.[97] But the issues are often exceptionally complex. For example, the variety of interpersonal and organizational realities facing contemporary lawyers, particularly in corporate settings, often raises serious questions as to who is the client, while the Code assumes the existence of the client as a premise of analysis. A

34 LEGAL ETHICS AND LEGAL EDUCATION

lawyer is often faced with the dilemma of whether to act as an adversary for one party to a transaction, or to serve "the situation" as "mediator and impartial arbitrator" between clients. These decisions dramatically affect clients who are deeply suspicious of, if not hostile to, attorneys citing conflict rules requiring the involvement of yet another attorney.[98]

(c) Confidentiality

Confidentiality in the Code has a long history and presents a host of interesting dilemmas. To an important extent the confidentiality principle underlies the conflict of interest provisions and a number of the problems relating to a lawyer's zeal for a client. The Code provision is broader in scope than the common law (often statutory) attorney-client privilege doctrine from which it is derived. The obligation to keep a client's confidences and secrets carries four exceptions to which a lawyer may have recourse: instances where the client has fully consented; those matters permitted under the DRs or required by law or court order; the intention of a client to commit a crime and the information necessary to prevent it; whatever is necessary to establish or collect a fee or defend against an accusation of wrongful conduct.[99] The blatantly self-serving nature of this last exception[100] is restrained in practice by the sound business reason that lawyers do not ordinarily flaunt confidences in their efforts to collect a fee. The first is hardly an exception at all, but rather a process for using information on a client's behalf. The other two exceptions (relating to intentions to commit a crime and the matters permitted by law or DR) create a confusing no-man's-land in which attorneys have enormous leeway to remain silent, although in possession of information that is extremely damaging to others, or to reveal the most trivial of client "crimes" or frauds.[101] Needless to say, the exploration of these fundamentally permissive "rules" generates intense classroom expressions of the conflict between ordinary moral perspectives and the role-morality of the attorney.

One of the great weaknesses of the Code is its strong orientation toward litigation problems. The Code remains in this respect a child of the Canons, despite the fact that in law practice of the 1970s only a small percentage of cases involve recourse to the courts. Although this weakness also affects many professional ethics courses,[102] a number of texts are beginning to focus on the ethical implications of other important methods of problem-solving by lawyers as counselors or negotiators, planners, and fact-gatherers.[103] The new ABA Commission to revise the Code is organizing the new version to address role-morality problems in categories such as counseling and negotiation, as well as litigation.

3. The Disciplinary System

One goal of many legal ethics courses is to introduce students to both the formal and informal enforcement of the Code. One of the most potent enforcement mechanisms is the power of courts to "disqualify" attorneys from representing clients, typically on grounds of conflict of interest under the disciplinary rules of Canon Five. This forcible removal from pending or active litigation can be enormously embarrassing, costly, and damaging to both clients and attorneys. Voluntary compliance mechanisms are not easy to assess, despite the large volume of bar-association opinions; the Code is, in all likelihood, not well understood by the bar in general.

Although only 500 out of over 430,000 lawyers in the United States during 1977 were publicly disciplined in any way,[104] the formal machinery for enforcing the Code is a staple in many courses, which describe the various committees, inquiry panels, and disciplinary boards established by state supreme courts to deal with attorneys accused of Code violations. Some states have adopted systems closely resembling the formality and due process requirements of the criminal law; others are more informal in their orientation. In addition to these procedural matters, some attention is at times addressed to standards in fixing punishments, such as disbarment, suspension, and various forms of probation and reprimand.

4. The Profession and the Delivery of Legal Services

One of the major goals of many courses and textbooks is to provide students with an understanding of the profession that is simply not found in the Code or its disciplinary procedures, that is, the theme introduced by Cheatham, the profession as an institutional structure. The realities of twentieth-century law practice comprehend a high degree of subject area specialization, social stratification of the bar, and complexities of law practice, economics, and management. Indeed there is little recognition of these and other stark organizational realities of contemporary law practice in the Code. Large firms and government and corporate law departments play an increasingly dominant role in absorbing new recruits, training young lawyers, and setting standards of performance in law. For example, the obligations imposed by the Code on the individual lawyer to extend legal services to those who cannot afford them, to engage in law reform, and to practice competently do not explicitly apply to the law firms and law departments that can most effectively address these obligations. A number of casebooks, therefore, undertake the task of describing the nature of the modern profession.[105]

Although there is general language in the Code about the desirability of making legal services fully available (EC 2–1), provision of legal services in organizational frameworks different from the traditional firm and individual practice has been recognized and inserted in the Code, largely through amendments. The tone is definitely one of grudging tolerance, if not distrust. Third-party financing through service and referral organizations is subject to a number of restrictions and cautions.[106] Canon Two ("A lawyer should assist the legal profession in fulfilling its duty to make legal counsel available") and its ECs and DRs consist primarily of elaborate advertising regulations developed in 1977 in the aftermath of the Supreme Court's decision in *Bates v. State Bar of Arizona*, holding unconstitutional the advertising prohibition in the pre-1978 Code.[107] The Code gives relatively little emphasis to organizational responses to inadequate provision of legal services to unserved middle-class and indigent publics. Here, the legacy of Cheatham and the Realists' criticisms, as well as the legal services developments of the 1960s, have had a strong impact on the available materials: many casebooks devote substantial space to these issues.[108] Some books focus on issues concerning legal services and the structure of the profession almost to the exclusion of lawyer-client relation issues.[109] Whereas analysis of different remedies and responsibilities for inadequate access to legal services by the American public could be described as an issue of distributive justice, the thrust of most texts addresses ways the profession operates in its contemporary institutional settings (admission to the bar, discipline, unauthorized practice, business-getting, fee-setting) and attempts, by classroom use of a text, to do more systematically what an older lawyer would provide the apprentice, that is, describe, often critically, the professional and organizational environment and give instruction in professional manners and customs.

B. Process Goals

What do teachers hope to accomplish through the course in professional responsibility apart from communicating some material on the Code, the profession, and the like? The response is sometimes implicit in the choice of subject matter. For example, the teacher who unabashedly trains students, in a one credit-hour course, to solve problems using the Code no doubt intends to assist students to pass the section on legal ethics on the bar examination. Most teachers, however, find a course largely limited to the stuff of bar examinations—the Code and disciplinary system—to be morally objectionable because it can, by and large, be taken as instruction in how far a lawyer can go legally before being subjected to the risk of discipline or trouble. Close attention to the ethical "bottom line" of the DRs and cynical treatment of the ECs is, in effect, to lower students' sights, to encourage contempt for a regulatory system that is largely permissive, and to trivialize the subject. Nevertheless, there is heavy pressure from students to take this path. Teachers from California, Minnesota, and Florida describe the introduction of a difficult ethics test on the bar examination in those states as creating student resistance to any course that does not focus almost exclusively on Code problem-solving.

1. The Consensus

Most courses go well beyond the Code, and, indeed, present a perspective critical of the Code. The purpose of these more broadly conceived courses is rather widely accepted: in the words of one of the more popular casebooks, it is "to sensitize" students to the ethical issues and obligations of lawyers derived "not from a revealed moral code but from the traditions of the profession itself";[110] sometimes this is expressed in terms of "insight" into the "problems of choice" of the practitioner,[111] sometimes as raising "the student's level of awareness of the issues."[112]

The ambitions of most instructors of this course include introducing students to the organization of the profession, identifying ethical problems (more broadly construed than DR problems), and developing analytical skills in the context of the traditional literature of legal ethics incorporated in the Code, cases, and bar-association ethical opinions. Virtually none of the materials present any formal analytical framework, for there is widespread recognition of a lack of consensus within the profession about many of the issues. The method, therefore, is "inductive": a lawyer and a student can only be sensitive to the issues involved, "see what guidelines the profession offers or fails to offer," and resolve these difficult cases as responsibly as he or she is able.[113] The teacher "sensitization" does not necessarily imply leaving a student in a quandary about the many problems of professional behavior raised in the classroom. The good teacher presents solutions and states how he or she would resolve an issue, while demonstrating tolerance for responsible opposing views.

Most ethics teachers are skeptical of the possibility that the course will result in changed standards of personal behavior, but express aspirations to have an impact on *professional* behavior. This distinction between professional and personal development is a problematic one. One teacher indicated a hope that future practitioners would, as a result of his course, wake up in a cold sweat about what they were doing. Morgan and Rotunda, for example, state in their teacher's manual that "we try to force students to examine their own basic values as they work through these problems." With the sensitivity aroused by the course, "an already concerned lawyer acting in good faith may become more professionally responsible, and in the aggregate, the level of responsible behavior by attorneys should rise."[114] Faculty members are aware that an enormous number of factors—family upbringing, peer associations, practice environments, the goals and motivations of the learner—affect behavior in practice, but they seek (just as faculty in other courses) to make an impact on the values of students within the context of their course. Strategically, of course, their greatest impact can come from casting the subject in terms of how to become an accomplished professional, but the implications are inevitably much broader.

2. The Activist Critique

A number of teachers are not satisfied with the limitations of the classroom for the teaching of ethics. Some fundamental differences separate the traditional law school legal ethics teacher from what I will term the "activist" position. Activists conceive of legal education as a much more important socialization experience than do "traditional" teachers. They believe legal education affects in major ways the "personality, the attitudes, and the values of those who are exposed to it."[115] A corollary of this assumption is that—although the role of the learner is critical—teachers have power to influence directly the moral development of learners in a variety of ways.[116] Those content with the current consensus, however, are skeptical of both this initial assumption and its "teacher power" corollary.

Activists insist that traditional classroom discussion of ethical issues falls seriously short of introducing a student to the complexity of ethical issues faced by practitioners, largely because a critical part of the subject is missing, namely, feelings or sensibilities. As Robert Condlin of the University of Virginia Law School writes:

> Behaving ethically is more difficult than thinking ethically because behavior is more complex than thought. To simplify slightly, in ethical dilemmas a lawyer is torn between immediate, personal interests, such as making money, appearing competent to peers, or avoiding discipline, and indirect social interests, such as helping others, or reforming or policing parts of the legal system. With some overstatement, the interest in personal gain is experienced emotionally, and the interest in social gain is experienced intellectually. This dichotomy exists, in part, because lawyer-client relationships are infrequently personal. Craft and politics, not friendship, are the motive bases on which most lawyers draw to mobilize talent and energy for their work.
>
> Sometimes self-interest and social interest are the same, and behavior that furthers one furthers the other. But often the two interests conflict. When this happens, as one would expect, emotionally experienced self-interest influences lawyer behavior more powerfully than does intellectual commitment to another.
>
> Lawyers do not see the issue of behaving professionally in these terms. They

do not understand how strong feelings of self-interest can blind one, even to the fact that ethical issues are at stake, or cause one to invent rationalizations for non-responsible behavior. Never having had that understanding, they also do not know how to use the mind (and its capacity for ethical analysis) to take control over the gut. Instruction in ethical decision-making and behavior ought to start from and be grounded in these data and experiences.[117]

Yet another more basic difference separates the activist and consensus approaches. Activists argue that effective learning or excellence in legal ethics occurs only by acting in the role of a lawyer. This perception has a long intellectual pedigree, dating back to Aristotle's insistence in the *Nichomachean Ethics* that the only means to become a just man is to do just acts.[118] A more modern authority is John Dewey whose "activist" epistemology posited that all genuine knowledge comes from acting upon the world.[119] Most practicing lawyers subscribe, at least viscerally, to such a learning theory based on their initial years of practice following law school.

We are, of course, back to the issues of moral development raised by Murray Schwartz's comments quoted earlier. Few would argue that the transmission of knowledge in the typical two-credit course on professional responsibility adequately addresses the dimensions of conduct and feeling in the acquisition of an ethical point of view as a practitioner. Lacking, in particular, are two kinds of learning that are particularly powerful methods of inculcating a professional ethic: imitation, or learning by identification with a practitioner (the so-called role-model); and the special conditioning or pressure of performing as a lawyer under obligation to a client.[120]

The argument concerns more than competing theories of moral development and learning.[121] Some issues of legal ethics, seldom found in current textbook literature, are emphasized and illuminated as priority issues from the activist perspective. Compared to the more spectacular dilemmas discussed in professional responsibility courses (Should a lawyer conceal a murder weapon provided by a client? Should a lawyer defend a client-defendant's perjury to the jury?) these are lower visibility, yet more pervasive issues.

The first is a problem fundamental to law practice and shared with most other professions, that is, the issue of professional dominance of lay people. The special expertise of the professional can be easily used to restrict, rather than to enhance, the autonomy and range of choice exercised by the lay client. Apart from one small section in EC 7–8, there is virtually no mention of this issue in the Code and none of the standard legal-profession textbooks focus on the problems it raises. The Code reflects a long tradition in the legal literature of attention to the limits of the lawyer's loyalty to the client. It is silent about what might be termed the limits of the client's loyalty to the lawyer. The presumption of the Code is that the threat to the lawyer's integrity is the serious issue, not the threat to a client's integrity. These are crucial matters with enormous impact on a practice: the management of the information flow to and from clients, decisions relating to negotiation and litigation strategies, mutual understandings of the counseling relationship, and the degree of paternalism, if any, which a client wishes the attorney to exercise.[122]

The problem extends well beyond lawyer-client issues. Except for the conclusion in EC 7–10 that zeal for a client "does not militate" against a "concurrent obligation to treat with consideration all persons involved in the legal process" and to "avoid the infliction of needless harm,"[123] fairness to other parties simply has not been articulated in the Code as an obligation or general standard for the legal profession.[124] It is a striking omission which reveals a strong utilitarian foundation to the Code.[125] The deliberate limitation of the lawyer's moral perspective to that of the client's interest is designed—provided certain limits are established—to foster the effective functioning of the adversary system and (presumably and ultimately) the betterment of society. The expectations of clients and others respecting the conduct of lawyers are thus made dependent on the demands of the adversary system.[126] Here, the profound bias of the Code toward the litigation model of lawyer problem-solving is most evident.

A third issue is competence. Most lawyers embarking on practice or a new "field" or specialized area run up against problems of their own competence, and seek out means (association with a firm, relationships with other helping lawyers, long hours of preparation) to reduce their sense of incompetence. But the economic pressures of law, except for the most lucrative and well-established forms of corporate or specialty practice, severely limit the amount of time that can be invested in a legal problem. Although attorneys' war stories have long illustrated examples of poor performances by lawyer opponents, competence has recently become a major issue in the legal profession, largely as a result of Chief Justice Warren Burger's provocative estimates of the high percentage of incompetent trial advocates, and his efforts (through the Devitt Committee of the United States Judicial Conference) to improve law school training in trial practice skills. The American Law Institute and the ABA Committee on Continuing Professional Education has undertaken a pioneering project to develop standards for peer-review systems for lawyers to address Code provisions that are a major addition to the old Canons:

> DR 6–101: Failing to Act Competently.
> (A) A lawyer shall not: (1) Handle a legal matter which he knows or should know that he is not competent to handle, without associating with him a lawyer who is competent to handle it, (2) Handle a legal matter without preparation adequate in the circumstances, and (3) Neglect a legal matter entrusted to him.

These provisions have proven to be virtually unenforceable because most disciplinary authorities ignore DR 6–101 (1) and (2) or feel there are insufficient standards available to measure incompetence.

Law schools have contributed little to research and efforts to develop institutional methods for recognizing and dealing with legal incompetence. This is probably a function not only of the difficulty of analyzing the complex (often noncognitive) factors that affect incompetence, but also because the leading schools in American legal education place most of their graduates in large firms where, because of the financial resources available for preparation and training, incompetence is presumed to be relatively minimal. Although law schools are unlikely, except in simulated exercises, to replicate the financial pressure of practice, they can create situations that allow students to address problems of competence in themselves, their adversaries, and their colleagues.

If the activist critique suggests that the lawyer-client relationship, the responsibility of lawyers to nonclients, and the complexities of competent performance are important, largely unattended issues in the study of legal ethics, it is a major additional step to suggest that law schools can effectively present these and other ethical matters in a form through which students learn to act as attorneys. Various activists choose different law school settings where the dialectical experience of analyzing matters of self-interest, competence, and ethical obligation can occur. Robert Condlin and Andrew Watson would use the classroom or seminar as a vehicle to engage students, although the degree of technical skill required to use the tensions of the academic social world for these purposes is formidable. The CLEPR position is that practice clinics provide much the best opportunities for these processes and analyses. Many law schools, however, have not confronted the difficulties of the clinical mode, which include: control of the nature, scheduling, and duration of cases to assure a replicable, generalizable experience within an academic time framework; financing of sufficient faculty to provide thorough student supervision and responsible representation to clients; and training of faculty to assure a reflective, analytical component to the activity of conducting a case.[127] The assumption of Bellow and Moulton in *The Lawyering Process* is that at the very least "role-playing" and preferably "simulation and practice materials" and "handling actual cases" are an essential part of their course designed to challenge the student "to reach beyond legal materials to find insight into [his or her] experience as a lawyer."[128]

The activist position is not tied to a single methodology or rejection of the value of classroom discussion. The activist case is that lawyering is an important *subject* for legal education from which students can develop insights into and preparation for—even practice of—the moral choices of law practice.

V. Recommendations

Prescription for change in the way American law schools teach ethics should begin with the obvious. The scene is a varied one, despite the dominance of what is described here as the consensus view. A large number of teachers are in the field; the pedagogy of law school teaching in general (including legal ethics) is a subject of intense debate and considerable experimentation. Legal ethics, already on a firm curricular footing in law schools, if only because of the demands of ABA accreditation, is growing in importance and acceptance, although in terms of prestige and attention it stands very far indeed from the front ranks of importance in the curriculum. Letting things take their present course probably means a modest advance for the immediate future.

A. The Materials for the Ethics Course

One of the respondents to our survey mentioned that one reason law professors resist teaching the professional responsibility course is that it is somehow "different" from other law school courses; it incorporates "nonlegal" materials. Many teachers react strongly to this "difference" by establishing what is surely a legitimate intellectual orientation for a course, namely restricting analysis to the politics, economics, sociology, and law of the profession as an institution. Another reaction is to proclaim that only the *law* of practice is relevant. A course that reviews the dilemmas of choice in the practice of law must, of course, review applicable law in the Code and elsewhere, but one of the main problems with critical issues in legal ethics is that there is all too little law.

Geoffrey Hazard describes the way in which some large firm attorneys approach problems of representation of multiple clients with potentially different interests involving the application of DR 5–105: they can give lip service to the Code, i.e., interpret the Code in the most cynical way to enable them to achieve their objectives; they can follow the Code; or they can pursue a course of "discernment in professional ethics," the disobedience dictated by conscience:

> [T]hese lawyers, at least in some circumstances, would rather bank on the clients' faith in them, run the risk of mistrust and subsequent recrimination and act, than take refuge in the Code's inhibitions.[129]

Many fundamental lawyering decisions turn on qualities of "affection, integrity, imagination, sympathy, and judgment."[130] A lawyer must use a bewildering variety of perspectives—individual, relational, impersonal, ideal[131]—to assess and act upon the world. The application of "law" to this complex web of facts and motivational claims is rarely determinative and often trivializing, i.e., it shares what Dewey calls the fallacy of selective emphasis of "favoring cognitive objects and their characteristics at the expense of traits that excite desire, commendation, and produce passion."[132] Legal ethics is not a *system* of laws, or rules or set of priorities applicable to the dilemmas and value conflicts faced by lawyers; it is rather a search for practical judgment or wisdom[133] which attempts to achieve some coherence among conflicting values and principles and concerns, together with awareness of the particular circumstances and a sense of the applicable range of shared experience, beliefs, relations, and expectations. Legal ethics also takes into account moral sentiment—those attitudes, reactions, and feelings which not only affect our actions, but the way lawyers evaluate, justify, and explain conduct and relate to people.[134]

This account of the proper subject matter of legal ethics is an activist one. The legal ethics course will always be viewed as a problem child in the curriculum, as a "Mickey Mouse" subject to students, until it engages the challenges in practice of the complex interactions of law, practical judgment, and moral sentiment. Attention to practice as an extraordinarily important intellectual problem is alien to the orientation of most American legal educators. A pedagogy that derives its materials from the unwritten modes of practice poses conceptual challenges to the predominant cognitive mode of American legal education.

1. Descriptive Ethics

One of the first tasks is to begin conscious research and the preparation of teaching materials in a "descriptive ethics" of how lawyers resolve problems of choice. How do thoughtful lawyers evaluate and act under difficult circumstances? How do they handle difficult clients and/or sensitive issues in terms of mechanisms of disclosure and consent?[135] How do they resolve a host of conflicts-of-interest issues? How do they handle the range of ethical issues generated in a wide variety of negotiation situations? How are their decisions affected by the different management, organizational, and financial settings of practice? Case studies of law firms (on the business school model) and negotiation and counseling "cases," similar to the litigation simulations created by the National Institute of Trial Advocacy,[136] could be effective both as teaching tools in the classroom and as a means of drawing attorneys into discussion about their practices, judgments, and justifications.

Take, for example, lying, which was the subject of a famous exchange in the early 1950s between Charles Curtis, a Boston lawyer, and Henry Drinker, the acknowledged leader of the ABA Committee on Ethics for a number of years.[137] Curtis's claim that "there will be situations in which a lawyer may be duty bound to lie for his client" was met with expressions of outrage by Drinker and others. It seems clear, however, that there has been relatively little systematic review of those situations and justifications alluded to by Curtis or others where lawyers openly deceive or consciously withhold vital evidence.[138] No literature exists, to our knowledge, on the practice of (which some suggest is widespread) and justifications for lying *to* clients, not for them.

There should be significant possibilities of interaction between philosophers and clinical law teachers or practitioners in developing cases and methods of analyzing these matters. For example, paternalism conceived of as a class of justifications may be a useful concept for analyzing a number of factors in the lawyer-client relationship.[139]

2. The Use of Theory

Another important task that could prove a matter of fruitful collaboration between lawyers and moral or social or political philosophers is the search for common values, i.e., systematic explanations of the rationale for professional ideals. The ABA-AALS Joint Conference Report[140] is a reasoned elaboration of what lawyers do and why the lawyer function is justified and important for society. It also contains one of the few attempts to articulate the basis for the adversary system, from which so much of the special role-morality of the lawyer is derived. One weakness in most of the current textbook literature is the failure to explore the rationale and limits of the adversary system as a basis for lawyers' conduct. This area deserves sustained attention, particularly the extent to which relevant distinctions can be drawn that affect the limits of lawyers' behavior depending upon whether the lawyer functions as a counselor and planner, negotiator, or litigator, or whether the lawyer acts in a civil ("private") capacity rather than in criminal defense and antigovernment modes.[141]

B. The Course

The basic course is an essential element of the law school curriculum, if only because the attitudes reflected in the Code concerning loyalty to clients, avoidance of conflicts of interest, and confidentiality are fundamental to an understanding, not only of legal ethics, but of the workings of legal institutions and lawyers. While a clinical mode of instruction might be desirable, classroom introduction to basic concepts and issues can surely be effective. A number of steps should be taken to upgrade the professional ethics course.

If the suggestions in Pipkin's study about the poor quality of teaching in legal ethics courses is in any way accurate, the AALS Section of Professional Responsibility ought to communicate to law faculty and administrators its low opinion of the lecture method which is still prevalent in many schools. The section could also act upon the recognition that there are (perhaps unique) problems in teaching the course for which some form of training program for new teachers of the subject would be appropriate.

A weakness of many present courses is that they are one-credit offerings. This is barely a gesture to the ABA requirement. The course is, or should be, one of the "building blocks" that enriches much of the rest of the curriculum. While most schools offer the course in the third year and many argue that third-year students are better prepared to discuss more sophisticated problems, such as the special difficulties of securities and tax lawyers, the views of Costigan in a 1917 article are persuasive of a different approach:

> The students we have had feel that the course should come early, preferably in the second semester of the first year, or in the first semester of the second year. They feel that, if instruction in Legal Ethics were given as early as that, the subject would receive the best attention of students, and they would be able to apply it in the classroom in the various other courses. . . . I gather that they have in mind opportunities to worry instructors in other subjects with ethical problems which, on reflection, they find those subjects conceal. Some students evince an envious regret at such lost opportunities. In any event, they have urged the giving of the subject before students reach their graduating year and are too much engrossed in the problem of how they are to make a start in life. They want Legal Ethics to be taught early enough to make a profound and permanent impression.[142]

The main argument for basic legal ethics before the third year is that the course is fundamental to any attempt to teach the subject pervasively throughout the curriculum. Without some student grounding in basic problems, the attempt of teachers to raise in class ethical issues peculiar to their specialties could be perceived as superficial and unconnected to the curriculum. Professional responsibility is rarely taught in the early years because of the competition to fit courses into the initial period of the law student's career when the intense work and attention essential to the success of the Socratic classroom is most likely to occur.

In the first year, many law schools make available special instruction, including small class environments, for legal research and writing, as well as appellate advocacy. Similar programs in the first or second year involving simulation and analysis of lawyer's tasks would be good settings for discussion of the attorney-client relationship, a review of what lawyers do, and exposition of the history and structure of the profession.[143] Another advantage of placing the requirement in the first or second year is that it indicates to students that it is a basic part of learning to be a lawyer, not a third-year afterthought which could not be fitted into the structure of the required curriculum.

C. The Pervasive Method

Despite the fact that it has always been touted as the most responsible way to teach ethics in law school, the pervasive method, i.e., conscious introduction of role morality issues into specialty subject courses, has generally been dismissed as ineffectual and has been confined to oblivion, while most faculties have embraced the single course as *the* method to fulfil the ABA requirement. Participants at a 1977 Detroit Conference on Teaching Ethics literally made no mention of the pervasive method, although it was a major subject less than ten years earlier at Boulder II.[144] Good law schools pride themselves on the fact that analysis of law-reform issues and possibilities does occur frequently throughout the law curriculum, but confining discussion about role-morality issues to one two-credit course out of some eighty to ninety credits required for the degree carries with it a powerful message about the importance of the subject. In fact, there are any number of contexts where discussion of lawyer decisionmaking would be valuable (e.g., family law, evidence, taxation, contracts, corporations) and where specialty problems enrich and enlarge the analysis and understanding of students beyond the basic course.

There has been little attempt to motivate faculty to assure that pervasive teaching actually occurs. For example, few, if any, schools have deployed research funds to support development of materials in ethics for use in their standard courses. Faculty are rarely hired with the specific task of supporting other faculty in the development of teaching materials.[145] In short, institutional resources are not devoted to providing the kind of incentives that are needed for the "pervasive" method to be successful. Here is one area where foundation or other outside incentive monies might prove useful. Once a number of teachers within a faculty, stimulated by study or research funds, begin discussing ethical issues as a respectable (i.e., funded) academic enterprise, the chances of pervasive teaching will be significantly enhanced.[146]

D. Clinics

Law school clinics can play an enormously important role in the teaching of legal ethics in law school, either as original courses in professional responsibility or as reinforcement of the basic course. Clinics can serve as laboratories or advanced courses in which students, acting as lawyers, explore the ethical dimensions of the performance skills they develop under the tutelage of a faculty-practitioner. Clinics can provide curriculum materials in ethics, for example, cases and situations that can be abstracted for classroom use in the professional responsibility course or for other law school skills and substantive law courses. The clinical and simulated skills programs are the curriculum area where pervasive ethical analysis should have the highest priority, and where its absence is perhaps most destructive. Instruction in legal ethics should be required of students prior to, or at the time of, their practice in clinic settings. Similarly, ethical study should be required of clinical teachers at some point in their teaching careers. Both clinical teachers and students need an ethical analytical framework within which to think about what they are doing.

VI. Conclusion

This review of the teaching of ethics in American legal education has focused on the design of legal education and the conventionally required ethics course. The most fundamental problem with the teaching of legal ethics is that it is part of the inherited structure of legal education and shares that structure's defects.

Virtually all commentators recognize that the lawyer must balance the interests of the client, the court and public, colleagues, and his or her own sense of integrity. It is also clear that the Code of Professional Responsibility is of little help in establishing clear priorities in situations in which these values conflict. There are a number of sound reasons for this lack of guidance: there is no clear consensus on many of these issues, and if there were, the delicacy, difficulty, and the range of situations in which lawyers confront ethical problems would be poorly served by a firm set of guidelines in a Code.[147] But if the goal of the course is, to use one course description, "to decide what kind of lawyers we want to be and what kind of profession we want to serve,"[148] there is a profound gap between the materials available either for an ethics course or courses in other subjects that raise ethical issues, and the world of decisionmaking by attorneys.

The reason that legal educators only scratch the surface of these problems is fundamental to the overall design of legal education: practice is conceived as something apart from education. The study of practice or the use of practice in legal education is severely limited. The required course attends to the "law" in the realm of ethical decisionmaking (as well it should) but the most challenging issues are left to the "discretion" of the individual practitioner. The professional responsibility course works around the edges of ethical decisionmaking by lawyers. What we most need are pioneering ventures of descriptive ethics and theory in the practice arena where the calls are close and the stakes are high. What kinds of reasons and relationships and sentiments are persuasive to those attorneys who in the exercise of their judgment take seriously the ethical dimensions of their decisions?[149] The strategic nuances, the institutional pressures, the personal relationships, the ideals and the concepts of the profession that are part of these decisions need articulation. The world of lawyers' "discretion" and practical wisdom needs mapping if we are to enrich our relatively primitive state of understanding of lawyers ethics in an adversary system.

NOTES

1. Schwartz is referring to the lack of specific guidance in the Code about difficult questions relating to the duty owed the client, such as keeping confidences ([DR-4-101 (C) and DR-7-102 (B)]) and taking what the lawyer believes to be unjust actions requested by the client (EC 7-8 and EC 7-9). Geoffrey Hazard makes a similar point in his ETHICS IN THE PRACTICE OF LAW 7-14 (1978).

2. Schwartz, *Moral Development, Ethics and the Professional Education of Lawyers* in MORAL DEVELOPMENT: PROCEEDINGS OF THE 1974 ETS INVITATIONAL CONFERENCE, 32, 41.

3. Goldberg, *1977 National Survey on Current Methods of Teaching Professional Responsibility in American Law Schools,* in TEACHING PROFESSIONAL RESPONSIBILITY: MATERIALS AND PROCEEDINGS FROM THE NATIONAL CONFERENCE 21, 23-24 (P. Keenan ed. 1979) [hereinafter cited as DETROIT CONFERENCE MATERIALS]. The 1958 figures are in Malone, *Our First Responsibility,* 45 A.B.A.J. 1023 (1959). There were, of course, only 110 ABA accredited schools in 1958 compared with 162 in 1977, but the percentage of the schools with an ethics course increased from about 49 percent in 1958 to 85 percent in 1977. The ethics course often goes under the title "Professional Responsibility" or "The Legal Profession."

4. *See, e.g.,* the textbooks listed in the bibliography, cited hereinafter by author's surname.

5. The ABA STANDARDS FOR THE APPROVAL OF LAW SCHOOLS requires under Standard 302 (a) (iii) that the law schools "offer and provide and require for all student candidates for a professional degree, instruction in the duties and responsibilities of the legal profession. Such required instruction need not be limited to any pedagogical method as long as the history, goals, structure, and responsibilities of the legal profession and its members, including the ABA

CODE OF PROFESSIONAL RESPONSIBILITY, are all covered. Each law school is encouraged to involve members of the bench and the bar in such instruction." The first sentence of Standard 302 (a) (iii) was first passed by the ABA House of Delegates in 1973. 98 A.B.A. REP. 154–56 (1973).

6. DETROIT CONFERENCE MATERIALS, *supra* n. 3, at 24, 48–49.

7. *See, e.g.*, Weckstein, *Watergate and the Law Schools*, 12 SAN DIEGO L. REV. 261 (1975); and Watson, *The Watergate Lawyer Syndrome: An Educational Deficiency Increase*, 26 J. LEGAL ED. 441 (1974).

8. Pipkin, *Law School Instruction in Professional Responsibility: A Curricular Paradox*, 1979 A.B.F. RES. J. Foundation 247.

9. DETROIT CONFERENCE MATERIALS, *supra* n. 3, at 54–57.

10. *See* Stevens, *Two Cheers for 1870: The American Law School*, in LAW IN AMERICAN HISTORY 405 (Bailyn and Fleming eds. 1972); and J.W. Hurst, THE GROWTH OF AMERICAN LAW 256–76 (1950).

11. O.W. Holmes, *The Use of Law Schools*, in COLLECTED LEGAL PAPERS 35, 36 (1920).

12. *Id.* at 37, 40, 47, 48.

13. O.W. Holmes, *The Profession of Law*, in COLLECTED LEGAL PAPERS 29, 32 (1920).

14. *See* W. Frankena, ETHICS 62–70 (1973).

15. *See* the brief historical survey and bibliography in Kaufman, *infra* bibliography, at 28–31.

16. J. Lieberman, CRISIS AT THE BAR 56–59 (1978).

17. Ohio State University College of Law, CATALOG Series 3, no. 6 (1898–99).

18. University of Maryland School of Law, COURSE OF INSTRUCTION 15 (1900).

19. Yale Law School, COURSES OF INSTRUCTION, 8 (1902–3); The University of Chicago Circular of Information, 2, no. 4 (1902).

20. Bond, *Present Instruction in Professional Ethics in Law Schools*, 4 AM. LAW. S. REV. 40–43 (1915).

21. *Id.* at 43.

22. *Id.* at 45.

23. Costigan, CASES ON LEGAL ETHICS (1917).

24. Costigan, *The Teaching of Legal Ethics*, 4 AM. LAW S. REV. 290 (1917).

25. *See* Committee on Legal Education and Admissions to the Bar, *Report*,

20 A.B.A. Rep. 377–82 (1897). G. Archer, Ethical Obligations of the Lawyer 35 (1910).

26. Special Committee on the Teaching of Professional Ethics in Law Schools, *Report,* 1928 AALS Handbook and Proceedings 158.

27. Committee on the Teaching of Professional Ethics in Law Schools, *Report,* 1930 AALS Handbook and Proceedings 149; 1931 AALS Handbook and Proceedings 157; 1932 AALS Handbook and Proceedings 143. *See also* footnote 5 *supra.*

28. Lochner v. New York, 198 U.S. 45, 75 (1905) (Holmes, J., dissenting).

29. *See* White, *From Sociological Jurisprudence to Realism: Jurisprudence and Social Change in Early Twentieth-Century America* 58 Va. L. Rev. 999 (1972) reprinted in G. E. White, Patterns of American Legal Thought 99, (1978); and *Legal Theory and Legal Education* 79 Yale L.J. 1153 (1970). For a recent bibliography on Realists' writings under the term "pragmatic instrumentalists," *see* Summers, *Professor Fuller's Jurisprudence and America's Dominant Philosophy of Law* 92 Harv. L. Rev. 433–35 (1978) nn. 3–16.

30. Llewelyn, *On What is Wrong With So-Called Legal Education,* 35 Col. L. Rev. 651, 662, 671 (1935).

31. *Id.* at 662–63.

32. Frank, *A Plea for Lawyer-Schools,* 56 Yale L. J. 1303 (1947).

33. Frank, *Why Not a Clinical Lawyer-School?* 81 U. Pa. L. Rev. 907 (1933). *See also* Gardner, *Why Not A Clinical Lawyer-School?–Some Reflections,* 82 U. Pa. L. Rev. 785 (1934); Fuchs, *The Educational Value of a Legal Clinic–Some Doubts and Queries,* 8 Am. Law. S. Rev. 857 (1937); and Mac-Namara, *Teaching Ethics by the Clinical Method,* 8 Am. Law S. Rev. 241 (1935).

34. 1932 AALS Handbook and Proceedings 32, 37.

35. Clark, *Legal Education in Modern Society,* 10 Tulane L. Rev. 1, 12 (1935).

36. Sharswood, An Essay on Professional Ethics 52–53 (1884).

37. Simpson, *The Function of the University Law School,* 49 Harv. L. Rev. 1068, 1072 (1936).

38. *Id.* at 1070, 1071.

39. *Id.* at 1082, 1083.

40. Fuller, *What the Law Schools Can Contribute to the Making of Lawyers,* 1 J. of Leg. Ed. 189, 193 (1948).

41. Mathews, *Foreword* to J. Stone Legal Education and Public Responsibility; Report and Analysis of the Conference on the Education of Law-

yers for Their Public Responsibilities, 1956 at 3 (1959) [hereinafter cited as Boulder I].

42. *Id.*

43. *Id.* at 98, Chapter IV *passim.*

44. *Id.* at 245–46.

45. *Id.* at 265–73.

46. *Id.* at 275–76.

47. Committee on Education for Professional Responsibility, *Report,* 1958, AALS Committee Proceedings 169, 172.

48. *See* Fuller's posthumous work entitled *The Forms and Limits of Adjudication,* 92 HARV. L. REV. 353 (1978) which borrows extensively from the Joint Conference Report.

49. *Professional Responsibility: Report of the Joint Conference,* 44 A.B.A.J. 1159, 1162 (1958). *See* the extraordinarily interesting critique of this document under the label of "purposivism" in Simon, *The Ideology of Advocacy: Procedural Justice and Professional Ethics,* 1978 WIS. L. REV. 29, 61–91.

50. EDUCATION IN THE PROFESSIONAL RESPONSIBILITIES OF THE LAWYER (D. Weckstein ed. 1970) [hereinafter cited as Boulder II].

51. *See* Rowe, *Legal Clinics and Better Trained Lawyers–A Necessity,* 11 ILL. L. REV. 591 (1917).

52. Bradway, *The Legal Aid Clinic As an Educational Device,* 7 AM. LAW. S. REV. 1153 (1934); Bradway, *Some Distinctive Features of a Legal Aid Clinic Course,* 1 U. CHI. L. REV. 469 (1934).

53. Frank, *Why Not a Clinical Lawyer-School?* 81 U. PA. L. REV. 907, 922 (1933).

54. Harris, *The Educational Value of a Legal Aid Clinic–A Reply,* 8 AM. LAW. S. REV. 860 (1937) and Piel, *The Student Viewpoint Toward Clinic Work* 8 AM. LAW. S. REV. 228 (1935). *See also* Stone, *Law Students and Legislation,* 7 AM. LAW. S. REV. 1138 (1934) (describing how students in a legal aid clinic use their experiences to bring about legislative reform to aid the poor); *but see* the note of skepticism expressed in MacNamara, *supra* n. 33 (clinical method trains students in professional etiquette, but cannot train them in fundamental principles).

55. Boulder II, *supra* n. 50, at 229.

56. *See* Pincus, *Council on Legal Education For Professional Responsibility, Past, Present and Potential Contributions,* in Boulder II, *supra* n. 50, at 327–32; Brickman, *CLEPR and Clinical Education: A Review and Analysis,* in CLINICAL EDUCATION FOR THE LAW STUDENT, 56 (CLEPR, 1973) [hereinafter cited as CLINICAL EDUCATION.]; and Pincus, *Legal Education in a Service Setting,* in CLINICAL EDUCATION 27.

57. Here I borrow from Alan Stone's excellent reply to a number of critics, *Legal Education on the Couch*, 85 HARV. L. REV. 392 (1971).

58. *Id.* at 417.

59. *See* Watson, *Lawyers and Professionalism: A Further Psychiatric Perspective on Legal Education,* 8 U. MICH. J. L. REFORM 248 (1975); Watson, *The Quest for Professional Competence: Psychological Aspects of Legal Education,* 37 U. CINN. L. REV. 91 (1968).

60. Bellow, CLINICAL EDUCATION, *supra* n. 56, at 374, 380, 384–85.

61. *Id.* at 391.

62. *Id.* at 396–97.

63. *Id.* at 410 n. 29.

64. PROFESSIONAL RESPONSIBILITY IN THE LAW, A CURRICULUM REPORT FROM THE INSTITUTE ON LAW AND ETHICS 12–13 (Gorovitz & Miller eds. 1977).

65. The one exception—the pervasive method—is discussed on pages 50–51.

66. Weinstein, *On the Teaching of Legal Ethics,* 72 COL. L. REV. 452, 455–57 (1972).

67. *Id.* at 457.

68. FELIX FRANKFURTER REMINISCES 19 (1960).

69. Costigan, *supra* n. 24, at 294. Only about 10 percent of professional responsibility courses today even bear the title of "Legal Ethics," DETROIT CONFERENCE MATERIALS, *supra* n. 3, at 30–31.

70. *See* n. 127 *infra*.

71. *See,* e.g., *supra*, ns. 3, 20, 27. The struggle has had a predictable by-product: There have been no less than ten general surveys during the last seventy years of the teaching of ethics in American law schools.

72. *See* Cheatham, *What the Law Schools Can Do To Raise the Standards of the Legal Profession,* 7 AM. LAW. S. REV. 716 (1932).

73. *See* Reed, PRESENT DAY LAW SCHOOLS IN THE UNITED STATES AND CANADA 255 n. 3 (Carnegie Foundation for the Advancement of Teaching, Bulletin no. 21, 1928); Stone, *The Public Influence of the Bar,* 48 HARV. L. REV. 1, 14 (1934); Weckstein, *Boulder II: Why and How,* 41 U. COLO. L. REV. 304, 308–9 (1968).

74. Watson, *Some Psychological Aspects of Teaching Professional Responsibility,* 16 J. LEGAL ED. 1, 12 (1963).

75. Kinnane, *Compulsory Study of Professional Ethics by Law Students,* 16 A.B.A.J., 222 (1930).

76. *Id.* at 224 and Weinstein, *On the Teaching of Legal Ethics,* 72 COL. L. REV. 452, 459–60 (1972).

77. DETROIT CONFERENCE MATERIALS, *supra* n. 3, at 36–37. Only 10 percent of all courses offered in the subject exceed two credit hours. There is no data on the number of students in a section. This is the author's educated guess.

78. *Id.* at 50–53. The 1978 AALS Directory of Law Teachers lists 291 current teachers of the course, of which 215 (or almost three-fourths) taught it for five years or less.

79. R. Mathews, PROBLEMS ILLUSTRATIVE OF THE RESPONSIBILITIES OF MEMBERS OF THE LEGAL PROFESSION (1966), published by the National Council on Legal Clinics and its successor organization, the Council on Education in Professional Responsibility, was the innovative and important first effort.

According to the Detroit Conference Survey, DETROIT CONFERENCE MATERIALS *supra* n. 3, at 44, three out of the four most widely used texts are problem method books (Kaufman, Morgan and Rotunda, and Redlich). Another problem method text, Aronson, has appeared since the survey. (*See infra* bibliography.)

80. *See* the introduction to Mathews, *infra* bibliography, at ix-x, and the discussion at the Detroit Conference, DETROIT CONFERENCE MATERIALS *supra* n. 3, at 61–80.

81. DETROIT CONFERENCE MATERIALS *supra* n. 3, at 42–43.

82. *Id.* at 44–45.

83. *See,* e.g., Aronson, *New Dimensions in Legal Ethics,* LEARNING AND THE LAW, Fall, 1975; Johnson and Ambrosio, *The Scale Program at Southwestern University,* DETROIT CONFERENCE MATERIALS *supra* n. 3 at 99; and *Innovations in Teaching Professional Responsibility,* DETROIT CONFERENCE MATERIALS *supra* n. 3, at 59.

84. Hazard, *supra* n. 1, at 16–17.

85. *See, e.g.,* Kaufman, *infra* bibliography, at 30–31 for a critical look at the so-called "clear cut distinction" between ECs and DRs, and C. Frankel, Book Review, 43 U. CHI. L. REV. 874, 877 (1976) (CODE OF PROFESSIONAL RESPONSIBILITY).

86. Frankel, *id.* at 880.

87. ABA Special Committee on Evaluation of Disciplinary Enforcement (1970).

88. Schwartz, *The Professionalism and Accountability of Lawyers,* 66 CALIF. L. REV. 669, 673 (1978). Schwartz's main purpose is to *limit* these principles to the advocate function, and to develop different principles for other functions of the attorney.

89. *See* Wasserstrom, *Lawyers as Professionals: Some Moral Issues,* 5 HUMAN RIGHTS 1, 13 (1975).

90. *See, e.g.,* DR 7–102(A) (1) through (8), DR 7–105, DR 7–106(A), (B) and (C).

91. Hazard, *supra* n. 1, at 40–42.

92. *See, e.g.*, ABA Formal Opinions 237 and 341.

93. *See, e.g.*, Lowery v. Cardwell, 575 F. 2d 727 (9th Cir. 1978).

94. DR 5–105(A) and (B). The consent must occur in a context where "it is obvious" the lawyer can adequately represent both. DR 5–105(C). The "it is obvious" test raises a host of problems.

95. EC 5–17, 5–18 and generally 5–14 through 20.

96. DR 5–105(D).

97. Thorough treatments are in Kaufman; Countryman, Finman & Schneyer; and Schwartz, *infra* bibliography.

98. Hazard, *supra* n. 1, at 43–86 is the best short discussion from a self-confessed "big firm" perspective.

99. DR 4–101(C).

100. Some argue that this exception is fully justified by traditional principles of agency. Meyerhofer v. Empire Fire and Marine Insurance Co., 497 F. 2d. 1190 (2nd Cir. 1974), cert. denied, 419 U.S. 998 (1974), is a widely discussed case in which a securities lawyer using DR 4–101(C) (4), delivered confidential information to the SEC and to a law firm representing the plaintiffs suing the company originally represented by the lawyer. Also relevant is Thurman Arnold's maxim, quoted in Hazard, *supra* n. 1, at 86: "If it comes down to whether you go to jail or your client does, make sure it's the client."

101. See ABA Opinions 202, 287, 341. Kaufman, *infra* bibliography, at 146–48, 152–53, and Hazard, *supra* n. 1, at 21–33, analyze the complexities of the intersection between DR 7–102(B) (1) and (2) and DR 4–101(C). See e.g., State v. Belge, 83 Misc. 2d 186, 372 N.Y.S. 2d 798 (1975), and *In re A*, 276 Or. 225, 554 P. 2d 479 (1976).

102. For example, the organization of Persig and Kirwin, *infra* bibliography, a popular casebook, rather closely parallels the organization of topics in the Code.

103. *See e.g.*, the pioneering effort by Rubin, *A Causerie on Lawyers' Ethics in Negotiation*, 35 LA. L. REV. 577 (1975), and Schwartz, *supra* n. 88, and the interesting textbooks by Brown and Dauer; and Bellow and Moulton, *infra* bibliography. Thurman, Philips and Cheatham, *infra* bibliography, contains a large section on the lawyer's nonlitigation work.

104. STATISTICAL REPORT, Standing Committee on Professional Discipline and Center for Professional Discipline of the American Bar Association, January, 1978 (Chart II).

105. Countryman, Finman, and Schneyer, *infra* bibliography, is particularly strong in this respect.

106. DR 2–103(D) (1) and (4).

107. DR 2–101, DR 2–102, and DR 2–105.

108. Mellinkoff; Kaufman; Schwartz; and Countryman, Finman and Schneyer, *infra* bibliography, are particularly noteworthy in this respect.

109. Thurman, Philips and Cheatham, *infra* bibliography, for example, devote only three pages out of a 533-page text to confidential communications between lawyer and client. Mellinkoff, *infra* bibliography, devotes roughly 50 out of 864 pages to this subject and about one half of the book to access to services, fees, rights to counsel, and the like.

110. Morgan and Rotunda, *infra* bibliography, at 2. *See also* Kaufman, *infra* bibliography, at xvii–xix.

111. Countryman, Finman and Schneyer, *infra* bibliography, at ix.

112. Redlich, *infra* bibliography, at viii.

113. Kaufman, *infra* bibliography, at xviii; Morgan and Rotunda, *infra* bibliography, at 2.

114. Morgan and Rotunda, REVISED 1979 TEACHER'S MANUAL TO PROFESSIONAL RESPONSIBILITY, PROBLEMS AND MATERIALS 7 (1979).

115. Stone, *supra* n. 57, at 422.

116. Bellow and Moulton, *infra* bibliography, at 28–34.

117. Letter to author, August, 1979.

118. NICHOMACHEAN ETHICS, bk. 2, chap. 4, 1105b, 5/12.

119. This is Dennis Thompson's characterization in THE DEMOCRATIC CITIZEN 60 (1970).

120. *See* R. Brown, SOCIAL PSYCHOLOGY 411–12 (1965); and J. Rawls, A THEORY OF JUSTICE 453–96, *viz.* 461 (1971).

121. Pipkin, *supra* n. 8, reviews a variety of competing theories of moral development. *See also* the authorities cited in n. 120. There is a literature of assessment and measurement of moral development of law students. *See e.g.*, T. Shaffer and R. Redmount, LAWYERS, LAW STUDENTS AND PEOPLE (1977); Thielens, *The Influence of the Law School Experience on the Professional Ethics of Law Students*, 21 J. LEGAL ED. 587 (1969) and unpublished work by Thomas Willging, of the University of Toledo Law School, using a testing instrument to measure moral development. The empirical findings of these studies are relatively inconclusive.

122. *See* Wasserstrom, *supra* n. 89, and the important contribution of D. Rosenthal, LAWYER AND CLIENT: WHO'S IN CHARGE? (1974).

123. *See also* DR 7–102(A) (1) (prohibitions against claims that merely harass or maliciously injure another) and DR 7–101(B) (1).

124. L. R. Patterson and E. Cheatham, THE PROFESSION OF LAW 73 (1971), are critical of this failure. For other criticism and suggestion for change, see the excellent article by Bellow and Kettleson, *The Mirror of Public Interest Ethics:*

Problems and Paradoxes, in PROFESSIONAL RESPONSIBILITY, A GUIDE FOR ATTORNEYS 219, 258–9 (including footnote 95), 269–70 (1978). The Canons were more oriented to the protection of nonclients than the Code. *See, e.g.,* Canons 16 and 18.

125. Cf. a rather different "utilitarian" approach, namely Bentham's famous attack on the principle of confidentiality in his RATIONALE OF JUDICIAL EVIDENCE reprinted and answered rather defensively in 8 Wigmore, EVIDENCE, § 2291. Charles Fried, in an otherwise unconvincing attempt to establish a nonutilitarian basis for a lawyer's loyalty to client, *The Lawyer as Friend, The Moral Foundations of the Lawyer-Client Relation,* 85 YALE L. J. 1060 (1976), sensibly points to certain limits to the loyalty of lawyer to client based on avoiding personal harm to another. Fried is more convincing about what might be termed the deontological justification for the special professional-lay person relationship in MEDICAL EXPERIMENTATION: PERSONAL INTEGRITY AND SOCIAL POLICY (1974) excerpted in Bellow & Moulton, *infra* bibliography, at 63–65.

126. At least one exception should be noted: The mention in EC 4–1 of the "fiduciary relationship" between lawyer and client. The lawyer is also permitted by the Code to refuse to act for a client when the action "seems to him to be unjust." EC 7–9.

127. There are also major structural problems, namely that the "top end" of the market for law graduates is not interested in a "product" with practice training other than practical training in research, writing, and legal analysis and argument. As Lortie has illustrated in his *Laymen to Lawmen: Law School, Lawyers, and Professional Socialization,* 29 HARV. EDUCATIONAL REV. 352 (1959), the potentially explosive oversupply of law graduates (which is, in part, a response to the social goal of making the legal profession accessible) is handled functionally by socialization *after* law school: lawyers are selected following graduation and "inducted later." Law schools that undertake to train students in practice matters—depending upon where they place their students— may be interfering with a relatively smoothly functioning market for law graduates.

128. Bellow and Moulton, *infra* bibliography, at xxiii, xxv.

129. Hazard, *supra* n. 1, at 10.

130. See C. Frankel, *supra* n. 85.

131. T. Nagel, *The Fragmentation of Value,* in KNOWLEDGE, VALUE AND BELIEF 277 (Engelhardt & Callahan eds. 1977).

132. Dewey, THE QUEST FOR CERTAINTY, 25 (1929).

133. This is an Aristotelian concept. *See* Nagel, *supra* n. 131, at 286–87, and S. Hampshire, TWO THEORIES OF MORALITY 17–39 (1977).

134. G. Postema, *Moral Responsibility in Professional Ethics* (unpublished paper for the Center for Philosophy and Public Policy of the University of Maryland).

135. A new casebook by J. Katz and A. Capron, now in manuscript, DISCLOSURE AND CONSENT, collects substantial written sources from both law and medicine.

136. The ABA apparently has underway such a project under the leadership, among others, of Bea Moulton.

137. Curtis, *The Ethics of Advocacy*, 4 STAN. L. REV. 3 (1951); Drinker, *Some Remarks on Mr. Curtis', 'The Ethics of Advocacy'*, 4 STAN. L. REV. 349 (1952).

138. But *see* the interesting philosophical exposition of Curtis's views made by Lon Fuller and Julius Stone, Boulder I, *supra* n. 41, at 121–22; and Bellow and Moulton, *infra* bibliography, at 84–91.

139. *See* Bellow and Kettleson, *supra* n. 124, "Problem No. 1" and related "Problem No. 2" and text. Problem No. 1 contains an interesting mix of issues illustrating unjustifiably "paternalistic" and "real interest" rationales.

140. *See supra* n. 49.

141. Important beginnings are Wasserstrom, *supra* n. 89 and Schwartz, *supra* n. 88.

142. Costigan, *supra* n. 24, at 292.

143. The University of Michigan's first year elective, Lawyers and Clients, designed by Paul Carrington and David Chambers, appears to be an excellent initial model for such a course.

144. DETROIT CONFERENCE MATERIALS, *supra* n. 3, at 65 (Donald Weckstein's comment on this fact).

145. Vanderbilt used a faculty coordinator for ethics for a number of years. *See* Boulder II, *supra* n. 50, at 124–27.

146. For a somewhat different point of view on the pervasive method of teaching ethics, see THE TEACHING OF ETHICS IN HIGHER EDUCATION: A REPORT BY THE HASTINGS CENTER, 1980.

147. An excellent discussion and elaboration of this point is in Kaufman, *infra* bibliography, at 613–17.

148. The course description in the Harvard Law School catalog, presumably Kaufman's. See his text at 619.

149. The methodology I believe will prove most successful is not one of surveying the profession or evaluating how unethical lawyers are, but rather to look at the reasoning of those lawyers who act "on conscience," whether in compliance with the Code or not.

Selected Bibliography

On the History of the Legal Profession:
Auerbach. *Unequal Justice*, New York: Macmillan, 1976.

Hurst. *The Growth of American Law.* Boston: Little, Brown & Co., 1950, chaps. 12, 13.

On the History of American Legal Education:
Stevens. "Two Cheers for 1870: The American Law School." In *Law in American History.* Edited by D. Fleming & B. Bailyn. Boston: Little, Brown & Co. 1971.

On Teaching Legal Ethics:
Analysis:

Pipkin. "Law School Instruction in Professional Responsibility: A Curricular Paradox," American Bar Foundation Research Journal (1979).

Schwartz. "Moral Development, Ethics, and the Professional Education of Lawyers." In *Moral Development: Proceedings of the 1974 ETS Invitational Conference,* 32. Princeton, N.J.: Educational Testing Service, 1974.

Content & Methodology;

Bellow. "On Teaching the Teachers: Some Preliminary Reflections on Clinical Education as Methodology." In *Clinical Education for the Law Student.* New York: Council on Legal Education for Professional Responsibility, 1973.

Keenan, ed. *Teaching Professional Responsibility: Materials and Proceedings from The National Conference* 61-179. Detroit: University of Detroit Press, 1979.

Meltsner & Schrag. "Scenes From a Clinic." *University of Pennsylvania Law Review* 127 (1978), 1.

Watson. "Lawyers and Professionalism: A Further Psychiatric Perspective on Legal Education." *University of Michigan Journal of Law Reform* 8 (1975), 248.

Weckstein, ed. *Education in the Professional Responsibilities of the Lawyer: The Proceedings of the National Conference on Education in the Professional Responsibilities of the Lawyer* 41–111. Charlottesville: University Press of Virginia, 1970.

Weinstein. "On the Teaching of Legal Ethics." *Columbia Law Review* 72 (1972), 452.

The Journal of Legal Education and *The Journal of the Legal Profession* often contain articles of relevance to the teaching of ethics.

Articles on Legal Ethics and Professional Responsibility:

Bellow & Kettleson. "From Ethics to Politics: Confronting Scarcity and Fairness in Public Interest Practice." *Boston University Law Review* 58 (1978), 337 (substantially similar to "The Mirror of Public Interest Ethics: Problems and Paradoxes," chap. 8 in *Professional Responsibility: A Guide For Attorneys*. Chicago: American Bar Association, 1978).

Callan & David. "Professional Responsibility and the Duty of Confidentiality: Disclosure of Client Misconduct in an Adversary System." *Rutgers Law Review* 29 (1976), 332.

Curtis. "The Ethics of Advocacy." *Stanford Law Review* 4 (1951), 3.

Frankel, C. Book Review, "The Code of Professional Responsibility." *University of Chicago Law Review* 43 (1976), 874.

Frankel, M. "The Search for Truth: An Umpireal View." *University of Pennsylvania Law Review* 123 (1975), 1031.

Freedman. "Professional Responsibility of the Criminal Defense Lawyer: The Three Hardest Questions." *Michigan Law Review* 64 (1966), 1469.

Lehman. "The Pursuit of a Client's Interest," *Michigan Law Review* 77 (1979), 1078.

Morgan. "The Evolving Concept of Professional Responsibility." *Harvard Law Review* 90 (1977) 702.

"Professional Responsibility: Report of the Joint Conference." *American Bar Association Journal* 44 (1958), 1159.

Schnapper. "The Myth of Legal Ethics." *American Bar Association Journal* 64 (1978), 202.

Schwartz. "The Professionalism and Accountability of Lawyers." *California Law Review* 66 (1978), 669.

Simon. "The Ideology of Advocacy: Procedural Justice and Professional Ethics." *Wisconsin Law Review* (1978), 29.

Spiegel. "Lawyering and Client Decisionmaking: Informed Consent and the Legal Profession." *University of Pennsylvania Law Review* 128 (1979), 41.

Wolfram. "Client Perjury." *Southern California Law Review* 50 (1977), 809.

Books:

American Bar Association, *Informal Ethics Opinions*, 2 vols. Chicago: American Bar Association, 1975.

American Bar Association, *Model Code of Professional Responsibility and Code of Judicial Conduct (issued periodically with amendments)*. Chicago: American Bar Association, 1977.

American Bar Association, *Opinions of the Committee on Professional Ethics (Supplement* 1968). Chicago: American Bar Association, 1967.

Callahan and Bok, eds. *Ethics Teaching in Higher Education*. New York: Plenum Press, 1980.

Carlin. *Lawyers' Ethics*. New York: Russell Sage Foundation, 1966.

Drinker. *Legal Ethics*. New York: Columbia University Press, 1953.

Freedman. *Lawyers' Ethics in an Adversary System*. Indianapolis: Bobbs-Merrill, 1975.

Hazard. *Ethics in the Practice of Law*. New Haven: Yale University Press, 1978.

Lieberman. *Crisis at the Bar*. New York: W. W. Norton, 1978.

Mellinkoff. *The Conscience of a Lawyer*. St. Paul: West Publishing Co., 1973.

Patterson and Cheatham. *The Profession of Law*. Mineola, N.Y.: Foundation Press, 1971

Professional Responsibility: A Guide for Attorneys. Chicago: American Bar Association, 1978.

Professional Responsibility of the Lawyer: The Murky Divide between Right and Wrong. New York: The Association of the Bar of the City of New York, 1977.

Rosenthal. *Lawyer and Client: Who's in Charge?* New York: Russell Sage Foundation, 1974.

The Teaching of Ethics in Higher Education: A Report by The Hastings Center. Hastings-on-Hudson, N.Y.: The Hastings Center, 1980.

Textbooks (asterisks denote texts where printed and duplicated supplements are available, reflecting current materials).
Problem method:

*Kaufman. *Problems in Professional Responsibility.* Boston: Little, Brown & Co., 1976.

*Morgan and Rotunda. *Problems and Materials on Professional Responsibility.* Mineola, N.Y.: Foundation Press, 1976.

Smaller-scale paperback problem-method texts:

Aronson. *Problems in Professional Responsibility.* St. Paul: West Publishing Co., 1978.

Mathews. *Problems Illustrative of the Responsibilities of Members of the Legal Profession.* Chicago: American Bar Center, 1966.

Redlich. *Professional Responsibility: A Problem Approach.* Boston: Little, Brown & Co., 1976.

Casebooks:

*Countryman, Finman and Schneyer. *The Lawyer in Modern Society,* 2nd. ed. Boston: Little, Brown & Co., 1976.

Mellinkoff. *Lawyers and the System of Justice.* St. Paul: West Publishing Co., 1976.

*Pirsig and Kirwin. *Cases and Materials on Professional Responsibility,* 3rd ed. St. Paul: West Publishing Co., 1976.

Schwartz. *Lawyers and the Legal Profession.* Charlottesville: Bobbs-Merrill, 1979.

Thurman, Phillips and Cheatham. *Cases on the Legal Profession.* Mineola, N.Y.: Foundation Press, 1970.

Texts Integrating Ethics Issues With Analysis of Lawyers' Functions:

Bellow and Moulton. *The Lawyering Process: Materials for Clinical Instruction in Advocacy* (with criminal & civil problem supplements). Mineola, N.Y.: Foundation Press, 1978.

Brown and Dauer. *Planning by Lawyers: Materials on a Nonadversarial Legal Process.* Mineola, N.Y.: Foundation Press, 1978.

Bloom, ed. *Lawyers, Clients and Ethics: Using the Law School Clinic for Teaching Professional Responsibility.* New York: Council on Legal Education for Professional Responsibility, 1974 (paperback).

Current Materials:

American Bar Association. *Formal and Informal Opinions,* vol. 1, 1969–vol. 2, 1973 to date (looseleaf).

American Bar Association Journal. A monthly magazine; contains summaries of professional ethics opinions and articles and columns of relevance.

Journal of the Legal Profession.

The National Law Journal and Legal Times of Washington, weekly newspapers on the profession, often contain articles about current ethical problems and opinions.

Bibliographies:

Education in the Professional Responsibilities of the Lawyer 359–401. Edited by Weckstein. Charlottesville: University Press of Virginia, 1970 (Boulder II conference).

Teaching Professional Responsibility 1275–1291. Edited by Keenan. Detroit: University of Detroit Press, 1979 (Detroit Conference).

Morgan and Rotunda. *Problems and Materials in Professional Responsibility.* Mineola, N.Y.: Foundation Press, 1976. Lists selected bibliographies under various subject headings in each chapter.

The Index to Legal Periodicals cites current articles, book reviews, and comments under subject headings: Legal Ethics, Legal Profession, and Ethics.

DATE DUE

PRINTED IN U.S.A.

KF
277
.L4
K45

Kelly, Michael J.
    Legal ethics and
legal education